The Best of Ryan O'Connell

The Best of Ryan O'Connell

RYAN O'CONNELL

Thought Catalog

THOUGHT
CATALOG
Books

BROOKLYN, NY

**THOUGHT
CATALOG
Books**

Published by Thought Catalog Books, a publishing house owned by The Thought & Expression Co., Williamsburg, Brooklyn.

First edition, 2018

ISBN: 978-1-945796-94-4

Printed and bound in the United States.

10 9 8 7 6 5 4 3 2 1

CONTENTS

How To Get Boys To Like You

Be casual. Be a free spirit. Be really physically attractive!

Be bold. Be desperate. Be you. (But not, like, the real you. A much better version of you — the "you" you'll never be but can sometimes fake if you have the right lighting and are wearing a flattering outfit.)

Meet a boy at a bar who smells like fresh laundry and firewood. Eye fuck him until you're exhausted and then make your way over to him. Yes, you can approach the guy first!!!! This is 2013. What do you think Susan Sontag was doing her entire life? She was working her ass off so you could approach a guy in some dimly lit bar. This is FEMINIZM.

Go up to this dude and be like, "So you took the STD test and it came back positive, huh?"

The dude — who looks like Aiden from Sex and the City except 30% more ugly and 20% more gay — says, "Excuse me?"

"The STD test. It came back positive, right?"

The man looks at you with utter confusion.

"I was just eye fucking you from across the bar and I'm pretty sure I gave you an STD. I'm sorry. Can I buy you a drink to make up for it?"

Ugh, that was such a good line. I have chills! The firewood guy agrees to let you buy him a drink, partially because he's intrigued by you and partially because he's terrified, and the two of you start talking.

You talk, you talk, you talk. You order guacamole. You talk some more. You imagine what he'd look like naked on all fours in a cabin in Aspen. You imagine his face as he cries to you in a cab and tells you that he has cancer. It all feels so real. Your relationship flashes before your eyes and it looks pretty good. There are a lot of brunches.

All of a sudden, you find yourself feeling overwhelmed with emotion at the bar so you start crying.

"Um, are you okay?" he asks.

"What's your name, sir?" You ask, dodging the question.

"It's—"

"Don't speak!" You snap, putting your finger to his lips.

You read somewhere once that men like girls who are spontaneous and a little bit aloof. So far, you've accused this man of having an STD, cried in your guacamole, and refused to learn his name. You think you're off to a pretty good start.

You dry your tears quickly and say you have to go. Men like mystery.

"I have to leave this instant!" you scream before running off alone into the cold, dark night. You assumed he would chase after you because that's what they do in the movies. You wait outside the bar for 20 minutes, hoping he would eventually come outside, but when he doesn't, you stomp back into the bar and ask if you can exchange numbers. Then, you tell him that his hair looks pretty.

You call the number he gives you when you're standing right in front of him to make sure it's not fake. Miraculously, it's not.

That night, while sitting in your dreamcatcher, you Google his name, which he had told you right before you left, and find out that he is an artist of some sort. Like, he draws pictures of bears and somehow they sell for $5,000. *Men are so weird.*

You text him sporadically, like little bird craps, throughout the week. It takes you about an hour to compose each text message, two if it requires a question.

Somehow he's into it. He texts back promptly, always with enthusiasm. You employ a team of social media experts AKA your best friends to analyze each text. The general consensus is that this man wants to be the father of your children.

You wait nine months to have sex with him because it's the average length of pregnancy, and boy oh boy, is it worth the wait. You read somewhere in *The New Yorker* that men don't marry sluts so you made sure to draw it out for as long as possible. To quench his thirst, you gave him three blowjobs a day and would occasionally let him do anal.

The day after you have sex, he gives you an engagement ring that's the size of Tommy Lee's penis. You cry. You scream. You dance in your underwear in the kitchen while listening to "Ain't No Mountain High Enough."

You knew this would happen. You did extensive research on how to attract men and it all paid off! Now you're getting married to a man who draws bears for a living and you couldn't be happier.

Sometimes though, when you're lying in bed together late at night, you forget his name. Is that bad?

"No," you whisper to yourself. "That's love."

5 Awesome Books For People Who Hate To Read Books

A few years ago I went to this party in the Financial District with my boss. I forget what it was actually for but there were a ton of "creative types" skulking about so my guess is that it was probably for the opening of some gay film series. A few minutes into the party, my boss left me alone to go do bossy things and I found myself fidgeting around nervously with my drink. Scanning the room full of people, I realized I knew no one there so I did what every bored and anxious person does when they having nothing to do at a party: I pretended to text people on my phone. After doing this for about 10 minutes, this psycho old guy (who I'm 90% sure was wearing a kimono) finally comes up to me and releases me from my misery. He asks me what I do for a living. I tell him that I'm a writer and his face lights up. He asks me what kind of writing I do and I respond, "I don't know. I write about gay stuff and having feelings and sometimes The Olsen Twins." Admittedly, I was being a little glib with my answer but whatever. I hate it when people ask me "WHAT DO YOU WRITE?" because no matter what I say, I'm bound to look like an asshole.

This guy didn't find my answer amusing though. He just nodded politely and started to grill me on my favorite authors. I told him my stock answer "Lorrie Moore and Joan Didion," but he wasn't satisfied with that.

"Do you like Tolstoy?"

"Um, no."

"Dickens?"

"Never read."

"Shakespeare?"

"I mean, sure?"

Disgusted, he hissed at me, "For a writer, you sure don't read. Open a damn book!" And then he sauntered off into the crowd, his kimono blowing in the wind.

Even though this dude was a stranger, he really hurt my feelings. The reality is that I *do* read. All the time. In the past two weeks, I've read four books and approximately 20 magazines cover to cover. I'm never not in the middle of reading something. I'm just not clutching my worn copy of *Wuthering Heights* and reading it by candlelight. My taste in books is more contemporary, less intellectual, more personal and journalistic. Shocker, right? The guy who wrote "What It Feels Like To Get Effed In The A" doesn't sit around reading the classics all day.

To be frank, reading these 1,000 page novels often bores the hell out of me. Like, I'm sorry I haven't read *Anna Karenina* yet but HAVE YOU? Who the hell has really met that chick anyway? She's so long! One day maybe we can sit and chill and get to know each other but for right now, she scares the hell out of me. Does that make me any less of a writer though? Does it give me less credibility?

The kind of books I like to read are the ones that snap, crackle, and pop off the page. They're exciting, they're funny, and they usually involve heroin addiction. I love them. Sure, they're not exactly dense reads, but I don't think a book's value should be determined by how difficult it is to get through.

So, without further ado, here are my book recommendations for those who don't necessarily love to read. I guarantee that these books will keep your interest and also make you rethink what constitutes as "good writing." (Note: I really only read books by gay men and girls. Sorry, straight dudes. Love ya, just #NotClearOn ya.)

1. *Ask Dr. Mueller: The Writings Of Cookie Mueller* by Cookie Mueller

For those of you who aren't familiar with Cookie Mueller, here's her bio. In the 70s, she served as John Waters' muse, appearing in classics such as *Female Trouble* and *Pink Flamingos*, before transitioning to writing and landing a gig as art critic for *Details* and penning her own column at *East Village Eye*. Beyond being a writer, Cookie was sort of a New York It-Girl. She palled around with artists like Nan Goldin, whose portraits of Cookie earned a place in her seminal book of photography, *The Ballad Of Sexual Dependency*, and basically did a ton of drugs and went to a ton parties. She represented the bohemian lifestyle, floating around the world on little to no money and having amazing experiences wherever she went. Cookie was no airhead though. Her writings, which are collected in this book, are equal parts hilarious and devastating. She provides sharp social commentary on what life was like in the 70s and 80s — a time when real artists resided in Manhattan and people were doing heroin like it was NBD. She doesn't glamorize it. She presents it exactly how it was. Reading her stories feels like you're hanging out with your cool aunt — the one that lets you smoke pot in the garage and gives you crystals from Sedona for

Christmas. Cookie died in 1989 from AIDS but her legacy is preserved in this book. Her spirit leaps off the pages and leaves you feeling nostalgic for a time that you unfortunately didn't get to experience yourself.

2. *Dear Diary* by Lesley Arfin

Lesley Arfin has the very important distinction of making heroin addiction sound hilarious. Okay, that's kind of a stretch. She definitely doesn't hold back when discussing the depths she sunk to while addicted to heroin but, even in the book's most depressing sections, Arfin manages to never lose her absurd sense of humor. I'll admit that I'm sort of addicted to reading drug memoirs — I find even the worst ones to be utterly fascinating — but *Dear Diary* is my favorite because it turns something that would ordinarily seem so inconceivable to many people into something totally relatable. You may have never been addicted to heroin but I bet at some point you *have* felt awkward, insecure, and hated yourself! Right? Well, then read this book. There's something in it for everyone.

3. *Dancer From The Dance* by Andrew Holleran

I usually say "No thanks, babe!" when it comes to reading gay fiction because the books always end up being so soapy and sensationalistic. *Dancer from the Dance: A Novel*, however, is a different kind of gay book. Taking place in 1970s New York, the book paints an engrossing portrait of homosexuality, one that manages to still feel relevant today. It's funny, it's sad, it's vivid, it's exciting, it's quiet. It puts all of my gay feelings into a blender and spits them back out at me. Please read if you're a person who's interested in general human emotions.

4. *A Good Man Is Hard To Find (And Other Stories)* by Flannery O'Connor

I majored in fiction writing in college, which meant that I had to read a bunch of short stories written by a bunch of straight white dudes. I couldn't stand most of them, not because I wasn't straight, but because they all seemed to say the same things: "I like whiskey; hate women; now let me describe this desert road for twenty minutes." By the time I got to Flannery O'Connor, I was in dire need of a woman's sensibility. I started off with her most famous short story, "A Good Man Is Hard To Find," and tore through everything else afterwards. Like I said earlier, I'm more of a contemporary non-fiction guy but O'Connor's prose was so attractive, I couldn't help but get obsessed. Her stories are #dark slices of Southern Gothic misery. Someone is always dying and there's always a strong religious vibe hanging over each of her stories. It's usually not my bag but that's perhaps why I love it so much. The best writers are able to make you interested in things you thought you couldn't care less about.

5. *Wallflower At The Orgy* by Nora Ephron

I was in the New Orleans airport reading *Wallflower at the Orgy* when I found out about Nora Ephron's death. The whole thing was surreal. I was just reading her hilarious thoughts on Helen Gurley Brown and now I was finding out that she had died. To make things stranger, I had just gone to BAM to see her speak in person about her writing and filmmaking career. I commented to my friend afterwards that Ephron looked so young. And she did. She looked to be about 20 years younger than her actual age, which is funny considering that so many of her essays center around her dissatisfaction with her aging appearance.

When remembering Nora Ephron's important contributions to pop culture, I feel like her successful film career often overshadows her remarkable talent as an essayist. *Wallflower At The Orgy* collects the crème de la crème of her journalistic contributions in the 60s and 70s, which range from diatribes about *Cosmopolitan* magazine to the food industry. Nora can be scathing while still remaining utterly likable in her writing, which is no easy feat. While lesser writers could seem bitchy and gossipy in their criticisms, Nora manages to get away with everything she says with a coy smile. This book is a great indicator of her talents and once you're done with this gem of a book, move on to *I Feel Bad About My Neck*, which is equally brilliant.

3

How To Tell If Somebody
Loves You

Somebody loves you if they pick an eyelash off of your face or wet a napkin and apply it to your dirty skin. You didn't ask for these things, but this person went ahead and did it anyway. They don't want to see you looking like a fool with eyelashes and crumbs on your face. They notice these things. They really look at you and are the first to notice if something is amiss with your beautiful visage!

Somebody loves you if they assume the role of caretaker when you're sick. Unsure if someone really gives a shit about you? Fake a case of food poisoning and text them being like, "oh my god, so sick. need water." Depending on their response, you'll know whether or not they REALLY love you. "That's terrible. Feel better!" earns you a stay in friendship jail; "Do you need anything? I can come over and bring you get well remedies!" gets you a cozy friendship suite. It's easy to care about someone when they don't need you. It's easy to love them when they're healthy and don't ask you for anything beyond change for the parking meter. Being sick is different. Being sick means

3

asking someone to hold your hair back when you vomit. Either love me with vomit in my hair or don't love me at all.

Somebody loves you if they call you out on your bullshit. They're not passive, they don't just let you get away with murder. They know you well enough and care about you enough to ask you to chill out, to bust your balls, to tell you to stop. They aren't passive observers in your life, they are in the trenches. They have an opinion about your decisions and the things you say and do. They want to be a part of it; they want to be a part of you.

Somebody loves you if they don't mind the quiet. They don't mind running errands with you or cleaning your apartment while blasting some annoying music. There's no pressure, no need to fill the silences. You know how with some of your friends there needs to be some sort of activity for you to hang out? You don't feel comfortable just shooting the shit and watching bad reality TV with them. You need something that will keep the both of you busy to ensure there won't be a void. That's not love. That's "hey babe! i like you okay. do you wanna grab lunch? i think we have enough to talk about to fill two hours!" It's a damn dream when you find someone you can do nothing with. Whether you're skydiving together or sitting at home and doing different things, it's always comfortable. That is fucking love.

Somebody loves you if they want you to be happy, even if that involves something that doesn't benefit them. They realize the things you need to do in order to be content and come to terms with the fact that it might not include them. Never underestimate the gift of understanding. When there are so many people who are selfish and equate relationships as something that only must make them happy, having someone around who can take their needs out of any given situation if they need to.

Somebody loves you if they can order you food without having to be told what you want. Somebody loves you if they rub your back at any given moment. Somebody loves you if they give you oral sex without expecting anything back. Somebody loves you if they don't care about your job or how much money you make. It's a relationship where no one is selling something to the other. No one is the prostitute. Somebody loves you if they'll watch a movie starring Kate Hudson because you really really want to see it. Somebody loves you if they're able to create their own separate world with you, away from the internet and your job and family and friends. Just you and them.

Somebody will always love you. If you don't think this is true, then you're not paying close enough attention.

4

The 3 Worst Hangovers of My Life

Hangover # 1: Trick or Treat!

The first time I ever vomited from drinking also happens to be my most traumatizing experience with booze ever. It took place on Halloween night in 2006 when I was a sophomore in college. I had gone to a costume party dressed as Andy Warhol (I had already lost my wig in the above pic) where I proceeded to get completely college-wasted off of a magnum sized bottle of wine and six JELL-O shots. Things initially felt fine and after a while my friends and I had decided to get a ride with someone to another party. To this day, I can't remember the name of the girl who drove us, which is unfortunate because after ten minutes of us driving, I began to vomit all over the interior of her car. Being a near stranger, she started to get really pissed and scream, "OMFG, MY CAR! MY CAR IS RUINED!" She quickly pulled over to let me vomit on the side of the road like a respectable drunk person but when I tried to get out of her car, I face planted myself on the sidewalk, curling up to the asphalt like it was a pillow stuffed with goose feathers. Two of my friends were with me at the time but they were positively useless. Also wasted, they were getting anxious because they were late to meet their coke dealer at the second party. My getting sick really put a crimp in their plans for the rest of night, which presumably involved doing tons of yay at a house party and having pointless conversations about social constructs. Since I physically couldn't move, everyone just stood around me and talked in circles: "So like what do we do? I told EZ Jeff that we would meet him in ten and he has the coke! Like we can't have him wait. He'll leave!" Luckily for them and totally unfortunate for me, a police officer happened to be walking by and asked if I needed help. Seeing lines of blow and coke breath in their future, my friends were quick to be like, "Um, yes! He's really sick. Maybe he has alcohol poisoning? Take him away!" Within minutes, an ambulance arrived to take me to the nearest hospital. Confused and still puking, I remember trying to make out the words, "Stop. Just drive me home and feed me water! Don't take me to the hospital! That's so expensive!" Alas, my pleas fell on a desperate cokehead's ears. They needed drugs and this was the perfect way to get rid of me. The rest of the night was really hazy but when I woke up the next morning, I was stunned to actually find myself in the hospital with an IV in my arm. Since I had never puked from drinking before, I assumed that I had alcohol poisoning and actually thanked my friends at first for getting me medical attention. It was only years later after a handful of puking experiences that I realized I was just wasted that night and needed to sleep in a pool of my own vomit on my bedroom floor like everyone else.

It pains me to say that my saga didn't end there. After the hospital sent me home in a pair of size 38 pants (I had vomited through my jeans and underwear) and a safari shirt, I found myself still wasted and wandering around my apartment complex aimlessly. When I finally reached my door, I was too drunk to put the keys in my door so I started banging to get my roommate to open up. She didn't hear me though so I decided to just pass out in front of my door with my size 38 pants down around my ankles. Naked from the waist down in the hallway, my roommate finally woke up and found me. I spent the rest of the day puking and calling everyone I knew to tell them that I had had alcohol poisoning and spent the night in the hospital, which actually sounded pretty cool to most 19-year-olds. Looking back though, I feel major rage towards my coke-y friends for pawning me off to the hospital so they could get high. Oh, and it took five years but I finally received a bill for the ambulance ride. It was $700. By my estimate, that's about five eight balls of blow.

Hangover # 2: Taxicab Confessions

I moved to New York City when I was 21 years old, which basically meant that I spent most of my first year here completely wasted. The first group of friends I had made were heavy drinkers and I would try desperately to keep up with their alcohol intake. I never could though. My body would just give up and end up passing out at two thirty in the morning while they'd be raging literally around my body until six. It had been two years since my Halloween hospital experience and I hadn't puked since, which made me foolishly believe that I would never vomit again. One night I really pushed things to the limit though by drinking a bottle of wine and four margaritas at El Sombrero—a Mexican dive restaurant in the Lower East Side that serves hallucinatory drinks. Sensing that I was heading down a dark path, I decided to leave my friends and take a cab home. With visions of baked ziti and drunk Facebooking dancing in my head, I got into a cab headed towards my place, which by the way, was only a fifteen minute walk away. The motion of being in a car, however, immediately made me feel nauseous and I ended up vomiting inside the cab. The driver immediately freaked out and pulled over, making me give him all the cash I had for "repairs." I then ran home to my bed, where I ended up spending the next 36 hours of my life. I literally couldn't move the next day. I vomited until 7 PM and didn't eat until a few hours later. I remember calling my friend with tears in my eyes being like, "Does it ever get better?!" To this day, that is the worst hangover I've ever had. I didn't exactly learn my lesson though. I spent the majority of that year vomiting from alcohol. It was only when I turned 22 that I realized how much I could actually drink. Now, like a real adult, I only vomit once a year and it's usually on my birthday.

Hangover # 3: Midtown Meltdown

This last one was caused by a drug hangover. No alcohol was actually consumed, which makes it super #dark. My best friend from California was in town and staying in a hotel in Midtown. Since I was living in the dorms at the time, I was stoked to get away from the smell of Kraft macaroni and cheese and fluorescent lighting for a few days and do fancy things like order room service and watch movies. The whole weekend managed to be relatively PG until the last night in which we raged with a capital R. Being 21 at the time, I was really into trying new things and being generally insane. After a hard night of partying, however, I woke up the next morning crippled with the most intense nausea I've ever had in my life. I spent the whole morning on the bathroom floor until my friend suggested that I eat something so we ordered room service and I crawled back into bed. A few minutes later, the room service dude arrived and placed the trays on the bed. Immediately after seeing my meal of scrambled eggs, I threw up all over it Exorcist-style. The guy looked horrified, asked if I was okay and ran out of the room. I spent the rest of the day vomiting, sleeping, vomiting, watching *Real World* and vomiting. I stopped trying new things after that.

Retelling these stories, I feel super embarrassed about my behavior but it also makes me aware of the progress I've made as a human being. All of my worst alcohol and drug experiences occurred between the ages of 18 to 21, which is when they should happen. Looking back, I can't believe some of the things I did but that's okay because these incidents *should* horrify me. If I didn't feel far removed from it, I think I would be having a serious problem. Growing up doesn't happen overnight and I'm sure I'll vomit again at some point but at least I won't end up in a hospital and think of it as a cool experience. Wow. Progress!

5

Things I Regret Eating When I'm Drunk

1. Pigeon

Last night, I got wasted with my boss at some fancy restaurant in DUMBO that only had, like, three things on the menu. It was one of those places that had a 10-page cocktail menu but when it came to actual food, my options were this: a certain kind of fish, beef tongue, chicken breast, and some type of meat I had never heard of in my life. I, of course, opted to get the chicken breast because it was a safe and reliable choice, but to my horror, the waiter told me they had just run out! (Who runs out of chicken, by the way? How do you just run out of that?) Confused and drunk, I stuttered, "Um, well, okay. What are the other options again?"

He ran through the aforementioned items on the menu and when he got to the kind of meat I had never heard of before, I asked him what the hell it was.

"Um, it's pigeon."

"What?" I exclaimed, nearly knocking over my wine glass.

"Pigeon."

Call me a Simple Sally but I had never heard of pigeon being served at a restaurant before. Is this some new bullshit food trend where pigeon is considered a delicacy? Pigeons are sick. They poop on people's heads! #NotClearOn us wanting to eat them now, other than for sick, revenge purposes.

"Well, what does it taste like?"

"Um, it's good. It's pretty game-y."

Ugh, game-y? GAME OVER. I can't do game-y. Game-y meat is sick. But, hello, I didn't want fish and I wasn't stoked on trying beef tongue. What the hell was I going to do?! (It sounds like a ridiculous problem but when you're wasted and don't like anything on the menu, it feels like a major issue.)

My boss nudged me and said, "You should get pigeon."

"What? No! Why?"

"It's good. I like pigeon."

Jesus, have people been eating pigeon on the DL all this time?! THEY ARE SO CRAZY. I can just see them rolling up to restaurants in their sunglasses and being like, "It's pigeon time, bitch. Get ready."

I don't usually listen to anything my boss has to say but this time, for some inexplicable reason, I trusted him and told the waiter I wanted pigeon.

"It's going to suck," I hissed at him across the table. "I hate you. You better give me a bite of your beef tongue."

"You'll love it. Seriously."

"Whatever!"

Then I went back to doing what I do best which is drinking white wine and waiting for food. It ended up taking forever so by the time it actually arrived, I didn't even think to proceed with caution. I dove into that pigeon like it was chicken.

Big mistake. The second it entered my mouth, I immediately

was like, "Dear god, this is a case of YOLO gone horribly wrong."

It tasted disgusting. Since it was a bougie restaurant, the portion was tiny, I only got like a quarter of a pigeon on my plate, but it was still difficult for me to choke down. Every time I would take a bite, I would have to take four gulps of white wine just to deal with the rubbery texture and bizarre taste. Lesson learned: Not everything tastes like chicken, especially if it's a goddamn pigeon.

2. Food that I've dropped on the ground

Across from my favorite gay bar in Brooklyn is a fantastic bagel place, which I'll often stumble into after a night of drinking to shame-eat. A few months ago, I was about to bite into this delicious bagel when, all of a sudden, I lost control of my grip and the bagel fell on the sidewalk. My first instinct was to scream and cry but I resisted because I'M A LADY. Instead, I looked around to see if anyone could see me and then scooped it right up from the dirty sidewalk. I'm usually a psycho about my food being contaminated but I didn't care at this point. Mama just needed to put something in her mouth and since the gay bar was a wash that night, a dirty bagel had to suffice! (And, yes, I call myself Mama but only when it feels right emotionally, spiritually, and physically.)

3. My roommate's food

Indeed, I'm that asshole who gets drunk and eats their roommate's leftovers. I am not proud of the things I've done but look, what do you expect from me? I don't cook and I live with a twenty-something Rachael Ray. The only thing I keep in the fridge is water and pills, so when I come home looking for a fourth meal, I'm shit out of luck! My eyes scan the contents of our fridge and I see no food that's mine. Then I focus in on a plate of delicious looking leftovers that belong to my roommate and go for the gold! I dig into it over the sink, all the while hoping and praying my roommate doesn't wake up and catch us mid-coitus. The last time I ate her food was a few days ago and I broke the news to her by calling her up and telling her that our apartment was robbed.

"What?!" she screamed over the phone. "WE WERE ROBBED?"

"Yes," I said, trying my best to sound devastated. "But it's the weirdest thing. The only thing the robbers took was your leftover pasta. Aren't we so blessed?"

I thought it was a funny joke but my roommate was annoyed. I took her out to a Rich Mom dinner the next day as penance for my sins.

4. Asshole

I have a lot of anxiety about my asshole. Like, I'm aware that it's a #dark place and I don't want to have to subject anyone who's not my proctologist to it. I, on the other hand, am totally okay with other people's assholes and have no issue with engaging in a rimjob situation. What I don't like, however, is when I'm doing it whilst wasted. The whole thing is just sloppy. I'm sloppy, the asshole is sloppy. It's not a good look for me or the asshole. In the future, it's best not to get an E.A.U.I.: Eating Ass Under The Influence. (Ew, I'm sick and going to stop now.)

6

The Summer Is A Wonderful Time To Die

When was the last time you really scared yourself? When was the last time you let yourself fall down the rabbit hole, fall so far down that you didn't tell anyone about it? You share everything, you tweet everything, you Facebook everything, but this was kept secret. This behavior was so frightening that you wouldn't dare acknowledge it to anyone. This self-destruction was only meant for you. No one else. How romantic.

Last summer, someone told me that the world was going to end. It was the Rapture, we were all going to fry on this chosen day at the end of May. Ashes to ashes, dust to dust, we all fall down. In order to prepare for this inevitable end, I let myself slowly dissolve into mush. Open the bottle caps and swallow it all down. The bitterness is going to coat the back of my throat but I won't mind because it means I'm going to be somewhere soon that's different from where I am now. I hate it here. I like it there. Please, get me there faster.

Are you around? Can you meet up? C'mere.

I woke up on the day of the supposed Rapture already dying. I had been chipping away at my body for the past month, killing its survival instincts, and replacing it with a warm expectancy that the end was near. I was planning on going to Brooklyn to meet up with some girls who had been preparing to die, just like me. I felt a comfort when I was with them, a sense of ease that came from me knowing that they were hurting just as bad as I was.

It was suffocatingly warm out that day. My hands were trembling. I went to the Lower East Side to meet up with a man who would give me the tools necessary to perish, but he wasn't there so I went to a movie theatre on Houston and sat inside a bathroom stall.

Buzz buzz, my phone vibrates.

I'm in Brooklyn. C'mere.

Okay.

I went. I gave him money. I swallowed his medicine. (Why am I giving *him* money so I can die?) The stuff wasn't lethal but it gave me a nice push toward the end. My hands were still shaking. I went inside a restaurant and asked to use their bathroom. I threw up in there and I'm not sure why.

(Who am I kidding? I always knew why.)

Leaving the bathroom, I somehow cut my finger on the door and blood started going everywhere. I walked out to the entrance and tried to act calm, like I wasn't the kind of person who uses a public restroom to puke and bleed all over myself. It worked. They bandaged me up. They gave me a free iced tea. I think they were scared for me, I think they could see that I had been half-asleep for the past month.

I left the restaurant. It was still so hot out. I met up with the dying girls with their bulging eyes and emaciated tummies and felt immediately at home. We lay out on the rooftop eagerly awaiting the moment when it all would go PLOP and we could just go to sleep for real.

They were so far gone. Were they even there? Was *I* there? I always prided myself on being the one who was most with it but now I was starting to question if that was still true.

We couldn't poison our bodies fast enough. I watched a tiny girl take too much in. *How is she still here?*

The sun was going down. My limbs felt like they were detaching, my brain was being hit with pleasurable waves. I imagined myself being at the beach with a boy suntanning and listening to some fuzzy music. I had to pretend because my reality was so far away from this image. I was so far away from experiencing any real euphoria or human connection, it was pathetic.

The end was near. The end was here. The end never happened.

Waking up, we realized that the Earth was just how we left it: taunting us, daring us to do something other than fall asleep.

Great.

The Rapture ended up not happening but deep down, I knew a shift had occurred inside of me. It was the beginning of the end. This day would mark my own personal descent into a Rapture, a Rapture of my own design and control. If it wasn't going to come naturally, I was going to do it myself, force it out, bring it to the surface.

I was going to make it come.

7

Don't Wake Up Alone On A Saturday Morning

Your life is changing in small, important ways every day. The structure is no longer holding, no longer able to stay glued together, so certain things are having to leave you when you're asleep. They're so quiet, so considerate when they abandon you, that I bet you don't even notice.

They call this growing up, or something similar to it. You wake up on a Saturday morning and realize everything has become unrecognizable to you. The gauze has been lifted! When did this happen? Oh right, when you were sleeping. They came in at night and started to peel things away from you like an orange. They were careful not to cut the center, they were careful not to let any juice drip on the bedspread your mother bought for you. They wanted your life to look familiar to you, didn't want to shock you completely, so they kept some things intact. Some things, not everything. Guess what's gone? Wrong. Guess again.

You woke up on a Saturday and came to the sudden realization that you were all alone, that everything you had surrounded yourself with Monday through Friday, all the happy hours and all the business lunches and all those technological noises you drenched your earbuds in: it all added up to zero. You feel like a fool, don't you? You played the game like everyone asked you to and still managed get to this place of complete and utter loneliness and alienation. Where did you go wrong? Do you need to send another text message to someone? Do you need to pay another credit card off or have another Great Night Out? What can you do to feel more connected to the things around you?

On Friday night, everyone was right next to you. There was Olivia and Taylor and Ethan and Josh and Michael and Sarah, and they were all here by your side laughing and drinking and taking pictures. No one left till the morning and you went to bed just as the sun was hitting your eyes. When you woke up, it was three p.m. and already dark out. You found out that, while you were sleeping, Josh married Olivia and they moved to the country somewhere. Sarah went to grad school and had a baby in New Hampshire. She's gone. She wrote the last chapter of her book and she'll never be relevant to you again. You wonder what happened to Michael. Well, let's see. You loved Michael more than what was good for you and after sleeping with him for five years, it fell down like a game of cards. You don't have the right to speak to him anymore. You lost it when you lost him. Say good-bye to that. Ethan is living in Portland and makes annoying Facebook updates about his life as a mountain climber and Taylor became a heroin addict. Just kidding! She writes books about organic farming.

How did this all happen when you were sleeping? How did you manage to sleep through all of these events? You were asleep and now you're awake but it's too late. Everyone else already went to bed and now you're just alone and awake on a Saturday morning and that's it. This is it. Never fall asleep again.

8

Death In The Time Of Facebook

The last thing Katie Wilkins—a 25-year-old graphic designer from Malibu, California who was found dead in her parents' garage on April 28th of an apparent drug overdose—wrote on her Facebook was "Me too!" It was in response to a comment a friend named Christina Montaldo had left on her wall that said, "I'm gunna love our weekend get togethers...hikes and bbqs. hells yes get ready!" Katie Wilkins "liked" the wall post and wrote the aforementioned response on April 27th at 12:58 AM. Less than two days later, her lifeless body was discovered by her brother.

I never knew Katie Wilkins personally. According to Facebook, we have two mutual friends—one of whom made a status update about her passing and that's how I found out about it. Kate Muselli—a fellow Malibu resident and a friend I had met through Livejournal when we were teenagers and eventually met IRL when we were both living in New York years later—wrote on April 30th, 11:21 AM, two days after Wilkins' body was found, "Waking up to find out one of your best friends has passed is not the morning I wanted. I love you forever Katie Wilkins. I dont even know what to say anymore. But I know I will miss you more then I have ever missed anyone." I clicked on her name to see her Facebook (I had some vague recollection of who she was from lurking photos on Kate's Facebook) and saw an outpouring of grief from friends and family on her Facebook wall. One girl had written moments earlier, "Hey I love you so much. I'm not sure if what I'm hearing is true. Please please call me sweet girl. I'm thinking of you." The fact that this friend had not been sure if Katie Wilkins had died, even after it was reported on Huffington Post and other various L.A. media outlets, strikes me as odd but it's also a testament to the pervasive role Facebook plays in young people's lives. Assuming her friend had already called Wilkins' phone to see if she was alive, her next logical step was to write on her Facebook wall because she knew that was a place she routinely checked. It seems morbid to use Facebook as a confirmation of someone being alive or dead but in today's digital age, it's become the most immediate and reliable news source about someone's life.

After I looked at Katie's Facebook, I Googled her name to find out how she died and, to my surprise, a bunch of articles came up. After I read one from *LA Weekly*, I understood why there was such intense media coverage: Wilkins had been found dead in her garage with no apparent trauma to her body and her silver BMW missing. With no clear cause of death and a presumably stolen vehicle, this could be a potential homicide which, in the affluent, safe community of Malibu, is almost unheard of.

Days passed with no new news but I continued to check Wilkins' Facebook for any potential updates. I also, out of morbid curiosity, went through her Timeline to get an idea of what her life was like. She wasn't the most active user on Facebook but she would occasionally check in places and would almost always respond to people's wall posts. In the last few months of her life, her friends had been writing that they missed her and wondered where she went. Katie responded to one of these inquiries on January 27th, three months before she died, with, "Just stuck in my house on the hill haha. Still looking for work. What you doing this weekend?" In her death, every little comment or "like" becomes an important marker for her existence. As someone who had never met Katie, I wanted to get a feel for who she was and this was the only way I knew how.

On May 7th, a woman named Liz Kat posted on Katie Wilkins' Facebook wall a quote from Steve Wilkins, Katie's brother who discovered her body. It goes as follows:

I'm Steve Wilkins, Katie's brother. I found Katie dead in my parent's garage during the afternoon/evening of April 28th. She died sometime between the late evening hours of April 27th and the morning hours of April 28th.

At this time I believe Katie died of a heroin overdose, the investigation revealed strong indications of this. Included in the toxicology report is testing for date rape drug, specifically rohypnol. I believe the heroin or heroin/rup was administered by another person. The investigation revealed strong indications that the injection was not self administered.

Someone was there at the home with her before she died; her car keys are missing from the home, her car is missing from the home, if OD then drug paraphernalia was taken from the home. Investigation revealed the house was clean of drugs/drug paraphernalia. Her car remains missing and no one has come forward with any information about it. No one has come forward about her whereabouts on the evening of April 27th.

After successfully unlocking her cell phone, I looked at Katie's phone log to check her txt messages for indications of her contacts and plans leading up to her death.

Chris Benton, son of Pepperdine University President Andy Benton, is the last known person to have been with Katie Wilkins before her death. I have text messages showing a planned meeting between Katie Wilkins and Chris Benton on April 27th at 8:30PM. At 8:33PM video surveillance from the Malibu Mc Donald's restaurant shows Katie, in her 1998 BMW Silver Z3, pulling into the McDonalds parking lot, Chris entering the car as a passenger, and just the two of them driving away. This is her last known whereabouts before she was found dead at our family home on April 28th.

When Chris Benton was contacted for questioning about his involvement with Katie on the night of April the 27th an attorney was hired for him.

I have indication that Chris Benton was entered into a drug treatment facility on April 28th. He has not been questioned; he has not made himself available for questioning.

This was a huge lead in the case and one that I had yet to see reported on any major news outlet. After that posting, friends expressed outrage about The Bentons' unwillingness to talk to the police. Someone wrote on May 9th on Katie Wilkins' Face-book wall:

I challenge Katie Wilkins friends and alumni of Pepperdine to beseige the face book page of Pepperdine to request President Andrew Benton to answer for his inaction and lack of leadership example by covering for the sins of his son Chris Benton who has a reputation among law enforcement and the Malibu community for being rotten to the core without any moral apptitude!"

Watching Katie's loved ones share breakthroughs in her case

and use her Facebook page as a way to jumpstart some grass-roots mobilizing was amazingly touching. In the past, I had only seen Facebook be used as a memorial for those who died. In the case of Katie Wilkins, however, there were a lot of unanswered questions. As a result, her Facebook not only became a place for her friends and family to express their sadness and share memories, it also became a way for people to unite and search for justice in the wake of her death.

A day after the posting of Steve Wilkins' statement on Facebook, The Los Angeles Times and other media outlets reported a new break in the case: Wilkins' BMW had been found in Woodland Hills and was being dusted for fingerprints. Detectives told reporters that the case was still considered "non-criminal" but that they would like to talk to Chris Benton, and ask him "such questions as: "Did you end up at her house? How did she end up dead?" Unfortunately, Benton has hired an attorney and is refusing to talk. He's also, as Steve Wilkins previously noted, in an undisclosed rehab facility, which he checked into the day Katie was found dead.

Benton's reluctance to share information about Katie's last moments hasn't deterred her friends and family from finding out what really happened. They've created a Facebook page called Truth For Katie with the tagline: "We want justice. We want the truth, for Katie." in the hopes that it will encourage anyone who has information about her death to come forward and share what they know. They've also created a petition at Change.org that's asking Chris and his father Andrew Benton to reveal any information they might have.

It's been two weeks since she passed away and nary a day goes by where I haven't checked her Facebook for updates about her case. Like I said, I never met Katie Wilkins but perhaps that's why I feel so affected by her death. Having access to her Facebook page and her comment history and photos deludes me into thinking that I do know her in some small way even if, in actuality, I haven't a clue.

I believe that, in many ways, Facebook has changed the way we grieve. I've never had anyone close to me pass away before but I'm not sure how I would feel about posting memories of the two of us on their Facebook wall. Kate Muselli, one of Katie's best friends and my friend from the Livejournal days, wrote me in an email that she finds looking at Katie's Facebook to be painful but also therapeutic. She explains:

I check it everyday. Knowing im not the only one who misses Katie, and that there are other people who loved her as much as I did, makes me feel not so alone. Looking at her pictures & reading her past posts makes it seem like she is still here in a way. I can look back on old comments she has written me, & things I have written her. I have posted on her facebook a few times since I found out what happened, and I think being able to release what im feeling, or say what im thinking to her makes me feel better. I just want Katie's memory and spirit to live on forever. She was one in a million.

I think about how I would honor someone's memory when they're gone and if I would be able to look at their Facebook and Twitter, or if it'd just be too painful for me. I see pictures of Katie Wilkins now, a girl who's my age and lives in the same city as my father, stepmother, and brother, and I think of her as someone I could've known. And then I look at all of the people who are heartbroken in the wake of her death, who write heartfelt condolences on her Facebook wall and talk about how much they miss her, and I grieve with them. Just seeing how loved she was, just being able to see this at all as someone who had no knowledge of her life prior, I'm able to join them in some small way and mourn this tragedy.

9

The Two Times My Father Almost Died

Two years ago almost to the day, my father almost died for the first time. I remember him calling me when I was out to dinner in Brooklyn with friends and telling me that he felt very ill. I was slightly drunk when I heard this news though and kind of dismissed it. He didn't seem to think it was that big of a deal either. He figured that it was just a bad case of the flu and even though he felt like hell, it would go away soon.

A few days later, I received a phone call from my stepmother telling me that my father had swine flu and was in intensive care at St. John's Hospital in Santa Monica. I was sort of in disbelief—swine flu seemed like a joke—but I took solace in knowing that I was set to come to Los Angeles in a matter of days. Ironically, I was going to L.A. not to see my father but to have my sixth and final surgery stemming from a car accident that occurred in San Francisco more than two years ago. I was planning on staying in a rented apartment in West Hollywood for six weeks and my mother was going to fly down from Northern California to take care of me for a few days. I thought my father was too. In fact, I had planned on staying at his house in Malibu for a while to be by the ocean after my surgery.

But this wasn't about my recovery anymore; this was about my father's. He took care of me when I almost died and now it was my turn to return the favor. I had no idea what kind of shape he was in but when I landed at LAX, I had a voicemail from a family friend crying and telling me to call him immediately. It turns out that while I was flying to California, my father had been told by a doctor that he had only days to live. After relaying the news to my entire family and leaving me a voicemail, the doctor came back and informed him that he had read the wrong chart and that he wasn't going to die after all. Oops! I'm so glad that I was in the air when all of this went down. Otherwise, I would've just lost my shit at baggage claim and been so angry when I found out the doctor was like, "J/K!"

Even though my father wasn't going to die in the next few days, things were very much touch and go. He had a severe case of pneumonia and could barely breathe. In the days leading up to my own surgery, I went to St. John's to see him and was ashamed to find myself wanting to leave the second I got there. Seeing him sick made me shut down completely. I wasn't the doting caretaker I had assumed I would be; I was a fucking zombie. Look, my father is basically my best friend. We hang out and go on vacations together for fun. We do dinner and a movie; we hold hands sometimes while crossing the street (I know, weird, but not) and genuinely enjoy each other's company. I could not deal with his mortality so I withdrew in a time when he needed me the most. I felt horrible for being a churlish child but I also didn't know how to change my behavior.

I had my surgery and everything went off without a hitch.

When I felt better, I would go visit my father in the hospital and laugh about how we were both spending the summers in some kind of rehab state. Oh, speaking of rehab, I should mention that the doctors gave me a lot of Percocet after my surgery. Like a lot. And I quickly discovered that it's really not a good idea to give someone who's dealing with the mindfuck possibility of death a boatload of opiates. From then on out, I would pop two pills whenever I saw my father and the drugs would put me in a protective haze, like I was in a cocoon. I felt awful going to see my father stoned out of my mind, but my coping mechanisms were shit. I didn't even want to get dressed in the morning. I felt paralyzed but the painkillers helped me get out of bed in the morning. Ew, this is so #dark and cliché but I really don't know how else to describe it. It wasn't *Intervention* status but it certainly was my own valley of the blah's.

As he spent more and more time in the hospital, I started to think of excuses not to go visit him. One day, I blew him off just so I could get stoned and go swimming with my friends and I felt so ashamed of myself. The level of my self-loathing that day was off the fucking charts and even though I knew what I was doing was wrong, I honestly felt like if I didn't have to see it, then it wasn't happening. I was shocked that this kind of emotional ineptitude existed inside of me though. It felt like an invasion of the compassionate body snatchers had occurred and I had no idea who this person was. The possibility of someone you love dying changes everything though. It can change you into a person you never thought you could be; it can change you into a person who's incapable of doing the right thing.

Luckily, my father survived. After spending two months at St. John's, he was finally released and made a full recovery. I was so happy that I finally let myself cry. I also promised myself that if anything like this happened again, I would be more available and not let the power of denial swallow me up.

Eight months later, I got another phone call and realized that it was a promise I couldn't keep.

I was driving to San Francisco and about to cross the Golden Gate Bridge when my father called and immediately told me that he had bad news. I knew that my father had gone in for a prostate cancer test, but we all thought it wasn't possible he would actually have it. Hello, he almost died eight months ago. Doesn't he have a Get Out Of Death Free card? He had just gotten his strength back; his lungs were better than ever. Couldn't the grim reaper leave him alone for just a sec and go harass someone else?

Nope, no such luck, he had prostate cancer. I was in disbelief yet again. Prostate cancer seemed more real, more permanent than a trendy virus like swine flu. Before it had always seemed like he would make it through the rain. There was always underlying hope because my father couldn't die of swine flu, okay? But I knew prostate cancer didn't fuck around. My father informed me that it didn't look like it had spread though and then he gave me a terrifying percentage of his chance of surviving. My dad doesn't sugarcoat anything. I have never met a man who actually was incapable of telling a single lie. *Liar Liar* starring Jim Carrey was essentially a documentary about his life.

I spent that weekend in San Francisco trying to have fun but it didn't really work. I was crying in bookstores, in friend's backyards, in a grocery store. I even stupidly reread *The Year Of Magical Thinking* by Joan Didion in hopes that it would tell me the secret to grieving—a secret I had neglected to learn the first time I read it because I didn't have to. When you've never dealt with death before, you're not actively seeking out the truths about grief, not trying to retain the stories of other people's experiences. All of this changes, however, when you have had someone close to you die (or in my case, almost die). Now, you're always searching for clues and for other narratives that aren't your own. In them, you hope to find an "aha!" moment, something that will make you better equipped to deal with things. When my father was sick and near death, I felt like a defective human and I wanted to know how I could fix myself. I wanted to be that person who performs well in a crisis, that person who everyone envies and admires. But I wasn't going to change overnight and I certainly wasn't going to have Joan Didion tell me what to do. That bitch is crazy!

To make things even more intense, my father had decided to have his prostate removal surgery in New York, which meant that he was going to be staying in my studio apartment in the East Village for three weeks. Even though I was happy to get a chance to be a part of his healing process, I was also fucking terrified. If anyone knows anything about surgery involving your prostate, the recovery process can be… messy. And I had to be prepared to see my father in very vulnerable positions. I was in that phase of my life where I would have to be stronger than my father. He was old and sick, and I was young and healthy. I swear, sometimes I think parents have kids just so they can have someone wipe their ass when they can no longer do it themselves.

Before my father had his surgery though, we decided to go on a trip around the East Coast for five days. I think it was a way for us to have a "calm before the storm" moment, but it also kind of felt like an attempt at having one last great memory together in case anything awful happened to him. Going into it, I worried about the trip having a bittersweet quality to it. Every time we would have a great laugh together, would we worry that it would be the last great laugh?

The trip turned out to be seriously amazing though. One of my father's great joys in life is taking scenic drives and some of the best memories I have of growing up is driving up the coast together and going all around California. The guy just loves the charm of old towns and, like, beautiful patches of grass. It was May when we set out on our trip and the weather was beautiful as we made our way though upstate New York and then to Connecticut, Rhode Island, The Berkshires, Boston, Northampton and, oh my god, Provincetown. I had always wanted to visit P-town because I heard it was just one beautiful strip of flaming homosexual, and even though going there with my father was sort of "WTF?!" I knew I had to go.

Surprisingly, my father loved Provincetown and Cape Cod the most, and our stay there actually ended up being one of the best times on the trip. I went swimming at our hotel while my father took a four-hour nap (old people are awake for a grand total of six hours a day, btw) and then we went to this amazing dinner by the water. Afterwards, we rented one of my dad's favorite movies, *The Last Picture Show*, and also watched *Michael Clayton*. Basically, my father likes three things: driving, eating, and watching movies. Oh, and sleeping. So this was his (and my) idea of heaven.

When we got back to the city, reality set in and I started to panic just like I did the last time. "Oh my god, I can't watch my father be incontinent. Oh my god, I can't see him that frail and *old*." But this was me manning up and getting another chance to be there for him in a way that I wasn't before.

When he got out of surgery, I went to go see him and he appeared to be in a lot of pain. My father usually has an insane pain tolerance so seeing him scream was an unsettling experience. He spent the next few days in recovery at the hospital and I made sure to push my issues aside and be there for him. I had to talk myself through the steps as if I had just bought a piece of furniture at IKEA and was learning how to put the fucking thing together. There were roadblocks in my brain and I had to navigate my way through them and create shortcuts.

When he came to my apartment, he was still in pretty bad shape but after two days of TLC and codeine, he was actually in good spirits and starting to take walks. Actually the funny thing about getting your prostate removed is that you must walk a lot. It's one of the only recoveries that don't involve "GET LOTS OF R & R!!!" No, you have to be on your feet and working that bod ASAP.

My father and I spent the next few weeks eating out, going to movies, and walking around the city. It was as if he didn't just have major surgery; he was just visiting me on vacation in New York. I knew I was doing right by him this time around. The first few days were admittedly hard—I wanted the experience to be over and done with—but I powered through. OH MY GOD, AREN'T I JUST SO STRONG? Ugh, I realize that this whole thing makes me sound like an emotionally inept brat. What I will say in my defense is that you never know how you're going to react to something like this until it happens. You think you know but you have no idea: This is the diary of…someone whose father just might die. It has the ability to derail the strongest people. I mean, I almost died too. I went through six surgeries and two years of rehab. You think that if anyone could've been there for my father, it would've been me.

But sometimes it's easier to be the one who's sick. You can focus on your recovery and put all your energy into getting yourself better. When you're the healthy one, there's only so much you can do. You feel helpless just watching someone you love die and you don't have something to put all of your energy into.

I'm happy to say that the surgery was a success and my father has been cancer free for over a year now. Having him almost die twice in a single year was extremely surreal, but it kind of forced me to become the person I needed to be for him. I can't even say that these experiences made me appreciate him more because I've *always* appreciated and loved him. What it did do was reinforce the fact that I want to be the best son I can be for him because he's always been the best father to me. And this is what happens when you get older. The roles get reversed and I just don't want to disappoint him or myself the next time I need to step up to the plate.

10

Here's To Getting Older

Here's to getting older. Here's to no longer being called precocious. You're expected to be smart now and understand how things work. But you liked knowing words no one else knew, words you learned in books no one else read. Specialness dissipates with every wrinkle, or so you think.

Here's to getting older in a society that cherishes youth and the "hot new thing." Here's to becoming a "cold old thing." Here's to burning your scalp to rid any signs of grey, injecting poison into your saggy flesh and lifting things on your body that just want to hang close to the ground. It's hard to know if you're doing things for yourself or if it's really for something else. Do you really despise pubic hair, worn eyes and ashy hair? Maybe you do. You probably don't.

Here's to getting older and loving someone who makes sense, to picking out a partner who will wash your underwear if you're old and can no longer help it. Your lover will be quite different from the ones you were with when you were younger. Those people didn't "do" accidents. They only did perfect supple flesh, no wrinkles and high sex drives. You were an able-bodied prize back then. Now you no longer attend the fair.

Here's to getting older and having a place that feels like a home rather than a temporary living space. Those kinds of places never felt quite as warm, did they? Growing up, you'd enter a family's home and wonder if you would ever get it right, if you could ever convey a sense of security and closeness with a home. You would study the knickknacks, the subtleties, the expensive china. This was the kind of home that always had band-aids, butter, flour, a good cutting knife. You remember cutting your finger in your apartment when you were twenty-two and having no band-aids, only some Polaroid film and tomato sauce so you had to let it bleed. It's okay though. You had blood to spare back then.

Here's to getting older and knowing stuff—how to reduce a temperature, having your own sickness remedies, saving receipts for your taxes, understanding health insurance and homeowner fees and 401Ks. Your mind is just cluttered with this knowledge of what to do when you get sick, laid off or die. You're preparing for that awful moment that could change your life forever. March to it, back away, approach with the receipts. "I have receipts for this heart attack. I have cards. So many cards."

Here's to getting older and feeling invisible. You enter a restaurant and realize you're the oldest one there at age 54. What happened? Where did everyone go? Florida? People don't look at you on the street anymore and check you out. They avert their eyes and keep walking towards a tiki bar. You miss feeling desirable. You miss being a target audience for an ad campaign that didn't involve an early-bird dinner. You want someone to sell you Diesel jeans. Please let someone convince you into buying Diesel jeans.

Here's to getting older and having memories that can stun

you like love. Here's to knowing all of your important friends for more than two decades. Life started to matter for you 20 years ago. You remember when your memory had only been vivid for the last four years. You were seventeen and could only think back to middle school. Everything before that was just a spec, a blur of bicycles and playing and scraped knees and tears and science class and your next-door neighbor who you used to play with. Life has meant something to you for so long now. Fuck.

Here's to getting older and having a strong sense of self. Things don't wreck you in the way that they used to. You don't spend Saturday afternoons hungover in bed crying about someone who won't return your phone calls. Those afternoons were wasted, just dripped away into a fast dissolve. You wish you could bottle those hungover afternoons you spent in your twenties and shake them up, yell and tell them to fuck off!

Here's to getting older and possibly creating someone else, reliving those moments through their eyes and loving them so much more than you love yourself. Yes, here's to that.

Here's to getting older and "getting" your mother and father. Here's to enduring quiet tragedies and getting off the roller coaster.

Here's to getting older and always being healthy. Health is the most important thing we have. You don't realize that until it's taken away from you and you're left with nothing. Seriously. Nothing. You're reduced to mush and life as you know it could be over. Cherish those limbs and unclogged arteries while you can, kids.

Here's to grey hair, shit, life, death, kids, tabloid magazines, Florida, Williamsburg, children, lack of sex, tumors, warmth, and receipts. Yes, here's to that.

11

How to Appear Cooler on Facebook Than You Really Are

Being cool on Facebook is an art form that I've mastered through years of trial and error. Here's what I've learned.

When it comes to being awesome on the web, it's important to remember that less is more. Think of yourself as an Internet minimalist, if you will, and avoid making status updates like this one: "Had a beautiful day out with the BF! We ate Thai food, and went to Target to look for new curtains. Now it's time to watch *How to Lose A Guy in Ten Days* in bed! Snuggle."

There are so many things that are uncool about this. First off: Go eff yourself because I'm single and starving and Thai food sounds amazing right now. Secondly: You're going to Target to pick out curtains and spending your night watching an almost-funny rom-com? We all do that. We all go to Target to pick up our face wash and deodorant and spend the occasional night in with our Netflix accounts. I mean, cool people can't be going to super cool parties and be hanging out with super cool people all the time. Sometimes they need to detox by having a night of eating pickles out of a jar and Googling The Olsen Twins. The difference between the cool and the uncool is that the cool person never talks about doing any of these mundane activities. It makes them sound just like everybody else and that's their worst nightmare. They are not like you, okay? They are golden gods who crap Polaroids and sweat Marc Jacobs perfume.

If for some reason, you haven't left your apartment in a few days or done anything noteworthy, you can write something like, "Having the worst anxiety. Taking a Xanax, burning sage and listening to The Cocteau Twins. Never leaving my apartment." This status works on so many levels of cool. Having anxiety, for example, is really cool. Being anxious and not knowing how to deal with things/life/boyfriends is in right now so it's totally okay to write about drugs like Xanax on the Internet. You can never write about coke or mushrooms or acid because that's just too real, but discussing anti-anxiety meds and sleeping pills like Ambien is socially acceptable.

Listening to The Cocteau Twins will always be cool and saying that you'll never leave your apartment is hyperbolic and therefore super funny. Everyone will know that you're mostly kidding and that you're just decompressing from your super cool fun stressful life.

Now lets talk about your actual Facebook profile. On your Interests section, don't write things like, "Hiking. Tennis. Laughing Till It Hurts. Hanging with my girls and getting crazy!" Instead, type in lower case letters (it's more whimsical) and say things like, "cashmere. sleepovers. goths." That's it. Only write three vague things that don't actually reveal anything about your personality. It will leave people wanting more and thinking, "Who is this person who types in lowercase and likes cashmere, sleepovers and Goths?" A cool person, that's who!

When it comes to the music section, keep it similarly short and sweet. You need to list two hip bands next to a mainstream one. Write something like, "the slits. tiger trap. katy perry." because you know what's cooler than a cool person liking cool bands? A cool person liking an uncool artist. It's just so... unexpected.

Lets talk about your photos. If you really want to be dedicated, you'll only make your profile pictures visible. In this technological age, you can't trust that your best friend Chloe isn't going to tag a photo of you drunk and eating a hot dog. (Remember that Chloe secretly hates you and wants to see you fail.)

But I understand that most cool kids are too narcissistic for that and they need their friends to see any and all photos of them dancing in that downtown club doing coke off of Vincent Gallo's penis. (Just kidding on that last part. The Internet doesn't know you do coke.)

Just be very particular about which photos stay tagged. Don't exceed over 500 because it makes you look like a desperate socialite. De-tag photos taken with a cheap digital camera. Allow only Polaroids, Lomography, and photos taken with a Yashica T4.

Let these photos project a sense of superiority and effort-lessness and always keep the following pictures tagged: You on yachts, eating In N' Out on a sidewalk outside of a club, hanging out with your fabulous best friend who equals you in coolness (in reality, she might be a sociopath nightmare but you guys look great together in photos), the occasional "I'm real and have a family" photo of you and your niece, holding a champagne bottle, talking on your Blackberry in a cab, hiking in Los Angeles in a crop-top to show that you're healthy and exercise and don't do too many drugs. Last but not least: any and all photos of you looking expensive.

So that's it. You're cool on Facebook now. Have fun but also be careful. One photo of you holding a nondescript red cup of booze with the friends from your "old life" and you're back to writing about eating Thai food with your boyfriend.

12

How To Die On New Year's Eve

I almost slept through New Year's Eve last year.

It's embarrassing, I've actually never told anyone this before, but fuck it, here it is. I fell asleep because earlier that day, I had taken drugs — what else? — and ran around San Francisco with my best friend to prepare for the night's festivities. After a couple hours had passed, I was finding it increasingly hard to stay awake so I told my friend, "I'm going home to take a disco nap. Meet me at my place at 9:30 p.m. and we'll go to the party together?"

Yes, yes, okay perfect, love you, see you tonight.

So I went home and I passed out. My body felt like a thousand pounds, everything felt heavy, the Earth felt heavy, and when I slept, I felt dead. I was dead.

Side note about drugs: THEY ARE REAL. THEY WILL KNOCK YOUR ASS OUT. THEY DO NOT ASK FOR YOUR PERMISSION TO DO ANYTHING. THEY RAN OUT OF FUCKS TO GIVE A LONG TIME AGO.

I had closed my eyes when it was still light out and by the time I opened them again, the room was pitch black and I was too scared to look at my phone because I knew that it would just say "Fuck-up O'Clock." It was late. Way too late.

In fact, it was 10:45 p.m. A mere 75 minutes before it was to be 2012. People were no doubt already celebrating at their designated party spots, getting drunk and laughing with their loved ones. Me? I was just coming to from a drug-induced coma in a dark empty house. In retrospect, I don't think my life could've felt more like nothing than it did in that moment.

I had a bunch of missed calls and voicemails from my friend I was supposed to meet (people don't leave voicemails anymore unless they are concerned that you're dead) and I had to start immediately getting dressed if I ever wanted to make it to the house party I had agreed to go to. People were waiting for me. Right now my friends were probably crowded around a kitchen at someone's house in Noe Valley wearing their sequined dresses and starting to seriously worry about my whereabouts.

"Where is Ryan?" one would ask. "You can't just show up late to a New Year's Eve party. It's literally the one party a year you have to be on time for."

As a culture, we believe that how we spend New Year's Eve sets the tone for the rest of the year. And if that was the case, 2012 was going to be the worst fucking year of my life.

I knew that couldn't be true though. Nothing could've been worse than 2011. 2011 was all about looking good on the outside, thriving, receiving emails from friends and family that said "Go you! It looks like you're doing so well! Congratulations!", and doing face masks and smelling nice to cover up my rotting corpse. Basically tricking everyone into thinking that I was this picture of success when I was really just getting deader by the minute. Ha ha, joke's on... you? Me? Who can tell anymore.

Wait, do you know how easy it is to trick people into thinking you're alive when you're actually withering away? It's disturbingly simple. You should try it. Honest. It will make your bones freeze. It will shock you how badly people just want to know you're doing fine so they have one less thing to worry about. It will shock you to see the lengths they'll go to insure that your narrative doesn't change and therefore needlessly complicate their lives.

With an hour and fifteen minutes haunting me like a doomsday clock, I got my shit together at a rapid speed (nothing like facing the potential judgment from your friends to light a fire under your ass, am I right?) and called my friend, fiercely apologetic, explaining that my disco nap had accidentally bled over into the 80s. It became more like a synthesizer nap!

See? I'm joking. I'm normal. Look at me! This is not the face of a man who almost sleeps through New Year's. You must've had me confused me with someone else, someone less capable of telling a joke.

My friends bought my story of me just being SO SLEEPY because I was doing so well and when you're doing so well you don't typically do things that would harm you, right?

I came to the party and did my best impression of a functioning human being. It was great. Best one I've ever done. I didn't drink because my stomach still felt coated with drugs and I didn't want to make things worse. I stayed until 4 a.m., dancing and laughing and chatting and minding the social cues, developing a rhythm like I was a conductor and this house party was my unknowing symphony. If any of the night had felt real to me, I could tell you that the evening was sooo fun. But since it all felt like a job, it will just be remembered as an inconvenience, another thing that got in the way of my downfall.

I'm telling you this not to share a story about me being high on drugs because drugs are boring and can usually be interchangeable with something equally as devastating. This is more of a story about the roles we feel like we have to play in order to make it through. When my life began to take shape in some ways, when people saw me as someone who was "doing great," I felt the need to go off script for a moment. I wanted to challenge everything I knew about my existence and screw with it until I could no longer tell who or what was in control anymore.

I'm also telling you this to let you know that it is distinctly possible to change everything you know about your life in a single year. 365 days. 365 moments that chip away or, in some cases, rebuild everything you once knew. Don't believe me? Take drugs, fall asleep, almost miss a holiday, and see where you're at a year later. New Year's Eve is almost two weeks away and this year I intend on showing up on time and no longer pretending. It's just easier that way.

13

5 Things That Smell Amazing And Will Make Lots Of People Want To Have Sex With You

Okay, I don't know if this is just me getting older or whatever, but lately I've become obsessed with making my home and body smell amazing. Like I want to walk into my apartment and be in awe of the wondrous smells that are wafting through the hallway. "Who is this person who has made such an elegant and chic smelling home for themselves?! They must be really stable and have it together!" In the past six months, any spare cash I've had has gone straight to buying candles and various perfumes and colognes, and I think I've finally succeeded in creating a utopia of smells. My friends now come over and feel like worthless screw ups because I've made such a warm and cozy smelling apartment while theirs still smells like last night's party. Suckers!

I want to impart my newfound wisdom to all of the readers who want their apartment to stop smelling like One Night Stand and Regret. Listen carefully, grasshoppers.

1. Nag Champa Incense

Stop laughing. No, seriously, stop and just listen to me for a second. When mixed with other scents (fig for example), Nag Champa really comes to life. I personally love it by itself but that's because I'm a wannabe stoner freak who likes to hang Jefferson Airplane posters on my wall and wear outfits that are exclusively tie dye. Nag Champa has a bad rep and deservedly so—it reminds you of your loser stoner boyfriend in college and watching *Family Guy* with the sound off—but I encourage you to revisit it and try to use it as an accent. Combine it with other smells and see what you get. It might just become your guilty pleasure. If you're that ashamed, just hide the incense burner and tell your friends it's a scent from your local organic co-op.

2. Baltic Amber by Voluspa

Baltic Amber is like Nag Champa but with a job and an Anthropologie wardrobe. It's an amazing candle that has notes of Amber, sandalwood, vanilla, and cedar. It's only like twenty bucks and it burns forever. I used to burn this stuff 24/7 and it made me feel like a grown up who was going places! It's also sort of sexy so feel free to burn it when someone cute is coming over. I don't know about you but I've been persuaded to sleep with someone based on how their apartment smelled. What?

3. Media Room by Lafco

I need to have a moment with this one because it's pretty major. So Lafco is a total rich person candle company. Their stuff retails for 55 dollars a candle (LOL) and each one is named after a superfluous room in a mansion. Sample ones include ski house (???), poolhouse, library, and, my personal favorite, media room. I ask for this candle for Christmas, and then I burn it sparingly, treating it like it's a rare diamond. I understand that 55 dollars is an insane amount to charge for a candle, but they're the only thing I care about these days. I'm single, don't have a pet and work nonstop—just give me this one pleasure.

4. Tuscan Leather by Tom Ford

Tuscan Leather is a men's cologne that legit smells like cocaine. Just Google it and you'll see tons of articles that say, "Tom Ford's New Scent = Cocaine?!" His rep denies the similarity and is all, "Oh my god, no, it smells like leather!" but no one's buying it. Tom Ford clearly went on a bender and then bottled that bender to sell it for $200 a pop, which is actually cheaper than a coke habit so whatever. As it turns out, the scent actually smells great. Besides reminding you of clenched jaws and pointless conversations, it's evocative of musky masculinity and sexy dirtiness. Buy this instead of doing coke. It's better for you and humanity.

5. Chinatown by Bond No. 9

Chinatown and I met under less than ideal circumstances. Last year, I accompanied my best friend to Saks so she could buy the fragrance. The price is truly frightening (something like $200 for 50ml) but I was content to live vicariously through my friend's spending spree. Things suddenly took a #dark turn, however, when the saleslady asked my friend how far along she was. "ARE YOU PREGNANT?" The room went still for a second as we both let the words sink in and then my friend responded, "Um, I'm not pregnant." My friend's body is a Latin sensation—very *On The 6* by Jennifer Lopez—but she, in no way, resembles a pregnant lady. Isn't it common knowledge that you never ask a lady if she's pregnant? I don't care if she's actually eight months along and looking ready to pop, it could be some weird tumor in her belly, so you're not allowed to say anything. Anyway, the woman felt so guilty that she threw in a thousand samples of the perfume. I have since guarded those samples with my life and only spritz it in my room when I want to feel like a 60-year-old rich woman with crushed dreams. The scent is truly dazzling. It smells a little bit like old lady at first but then it transforms into some spicy and floral aroma that smells like a mixture of patchouli and cinnamon. Since the scent is so feminine, I can only don it when I'm walking around my apartment in an Erykah Badu headwrap but maybe one day I will gather the courage to walk outside my door with it on.

14

5 Things That Will Make You Smell Even More Amazing And Get You Laid!

I'm going to have an honest moment on here for a second. Last summer, I was so vaguely unhappy, so living permanently in the bell jar, that I never wanted to leave my apartment. On top of being a hermit (or perhaps because of it), I was also stoned out of my goddamned mind for three months straight. I was like a pilled-out housewife but instead of having a hot rich husband and a large home in suburbia, I was pathetically single and squashing roaches in my bathtub with rolled up pieces of tissue. As far as aspiring pillheads go, I guess you could say I was less of a Karen Walker and more of a Kim Richards.

So that was a terrible time for me. Phew, thank god *that's* over. I will say though that one good thing came out of being permanently high last summer: I became *obsessed* with scents. I don't know if it was a side effect of all the drugs I was taking or what but all of a sudden, I just became fixated on everything smelling good ALL THE TIME. I think it was my twisted logic of being like, "Well, if I smell like a wonderful blend of amber, cedarwood, and vanilla, no one will EVER know that I took five painkillers today! What's that smell?! Someone who's not screwed out of their mind, that's what!"

I became such a hilarious parody of myself, going to department stores like a zombie and impulse buying 1,000 candles and perfumes (some of which were meant for 80-year-old rich women in Prada, not 20-something gay men in stained Hanes t-shirts). I would come home carrying all of these shopping bags that were clanking with the sounds of glass bottles and candles, all googly-eyed and insane looking, and scream to my roommate, "OMG, let's do a face mask and light some candles, hon!" My roommate would be like, "Um, k..." and then I would retire to bed, spritzing on old-lady perfume that would make my roommate retch, and feel like a glamorous delusional stoned diva!

Even though the times and my drug intake have changed, I have continued to be obsessed with perfumes and candles. Don't you know this already though, dear reader?! I wrote about it last year around this time exactly! But I figured an update was in order. In the past 365 days, I've scoured the ends of the earth (or at least gone above 14th street in Manhattan) in the search for the perfect scent and here are my latest discoveries. (Note: all of these recommendations are Formula does not parse $. I don't play around with those five-dollar candles that smell like apple crisp and Grandma's melted down chocolate cake, okay? If you're not cool with dropping $60 on a single candle, congratulations! You're normal and I'm insane! Everyone else, please come inside Ryan's scent factory...)

1. Chateau Marmont Signature Candle

While I was in L.A., I spent some time at the Chateau Marmont (which you'll be hearing ALL about, trust me!) and the first thing I noticed about the storied hotel was how good it smelled. Whenever I would float down the hallways (Because you don't walk at the Chateau, you float, natch), I would stop dead in my tracks and say to myself, "What is that wondrous scent? It smells like elitism and drug overdoses with a hint of gardenias!" I ran up to the front desk immediately to inquire about their candle and they were like, "Oh yes, that's our signature scent. You can have it for 5,000 dollars!" and I was like, "Sold!" I burned this candle all throughout my stay in L.A. and it made everything smell so warm, sweet, and musky. And it's actually not $5,000. It's $50.00, which is still terrifying but you have to make sacrifices for the things you love, okay? When I'm dead, just bury me with my candles.

2. Tobacco Vanille by Tom Ford

In my post last year, I recommended the Tom Ford cologne, Tuscan Leather, which legitimately smells like an eight ball of cocaine. Like, if I were a recovering cokehead, I think wearing Tuscan Leather would be considered a relapse. It's *that* similar. Just yesterday though, my bottle ran out and I met up with my friend Danielle who was wearing Tobacco Vanille and it smelled AMAZING. I remember dousing myself in it when I was at Saks last year and being like "no" but my senses have clearly changed. The scent is a sexy musk that is the definition of unisex. And, no, I don't mean unisex in the sense that only gay men and girls can wear it. I think Tobacco Vanille could work for anyone. I don't smoke cigarettes and HATE the smell of tobacco but the smell isn't overwhelming here. It works perfectly in conjunction with the vanilla and honey. The only bummer about Tom Ford's scents is that they cost a small fortune. The smallest bottles (which I go through typically in six months) cost 200 dollars! Tom, hon, are you out there? Can you send me a bottle of Tobacco Vanille for free? I swear I'll find a way to incorporate it in every article. "20 Reasons Why Everyone Should Smell Like Tobacco and Vanilla," "Thoughts I Had About My Ex While Wearing Tobacco Vanille by Tom Ford." The list could go on…

3. Fig Tree Candle by A.P.C.

Whenever I go to A.P.C. to try on clothes, I end up sobbing in the dressing room because I feel like fat Elvis. Luckily for me though, their amazing candles are one size fits all! I'm the biggest fan of the fig one. I could burn it all day long and be satisfied. I could walk down the aisle on my wedding day to a song I wrote called, "Me & Fig Candles: An Expensive Love Story That Doesn't Involve My Husband." You get the point. I love it. Diptyque makes a fabulous fig candle as well but I'm partial to the A.P.C. one, even if it does bring up painful memories of trying on too-small items of clothing in the store and having to ask for a size large. "Oh, um…" the anorexic salesperson tells me, "I think we have some in the stockroom…" IS THAT WHERE YOU KEEP THE REGULAR-SIZED PEOPLE? TIED UP IN THE BASEMENT? FINE, TAKE ME THERE, I WANNA GO THERE.

4. Aveda Shampure Candle

Ok, I know it's weird to burn a candle that smells like a shampoo but just trust me. This Aveda Shampure candle is PERFECT to burn in your bathroom. I would never dare bring it out to my main living room area (it's not ready for primetime, honey) but it works so well burning in the bathroom because the scent is so clean and crisp. Plus, it's where you wash your hair anyway so why not just have shampoo in a candle version as well? Retailing at $34.00, it's also the cheapest offering on my list. (PATHETIC, I KNOW. SEND ME TO EXPENSIVE CANDLE JAIL. IT'S A LEGITIMATE DISEASE THOUGH. HAVE SOME CUMPASSION.)

5. Orange Blossom by Jo Malone

I don't own this perfume myself, my roommate does. (I'm not that gay, you psychos!) But sometimes I'll wear it when I'm hungover because it smells so smooth and precious, like a delicate cloud floating over an orange grove in California. Sometimes you just need a soft, underwhelming scent that's sort of an added surprise. Ordinarily, I like to drown in cologne (as long as you're not wearing Ed Hardy rapist perfume, it's okay to use liberal amounts) but when my head is aching and I'm dry heaving, I need just a little splash of Jo Malone's Orange Blossom perfume and I'm good to go.

P.S. I can't actually guarantee that these scents will get you laid. In fact, it might hurt your chances, especially if you spend thirty minutes talking about your love of candles on a first date like I have. Oops!

15

7 Things You Should Know About Girls

I love girls and I like to surround myself with them as much as possible. I'm by no means an expert (I think I would need a vagina in order to be considered one) but I've learned some interesting things about them throughout the years. Warning: It sounds like I'm speaking for all women in this article (OMG, the title) but I'm actually not. I'm talking about my experiences and *my* women.

1. Some of them hate other girls for no apparent reason. This is the kind of girl who has a lot of guy friends and calls herself a tomboy. She claims to not have many girlfriends because she thinks they are so much drama and she only likes people who are chill. Yeah... I don't buy it. Do you? In my experience, these kinds of girls are just super competitive and feel superior when they're surrounded by a bunch of dudes—even if it's platonic. This goes against the message of the groundbreaking film, *Mean Girls*, which is that girls need to love each other! Otherwise, they're allowing

themselves to get teared down by men. Feminism 101.

2. Overall, girls seem to pay more attention than men. They pay attention to people's feelings, to social dynamics, to the temperature (it's too hot, it's too cold). They're in tune with the things going on around them. And thank god for that because these sensitive beautiful creatures just seem to get *it*. My best girlfriends are the most thoughtful empathetic ladies ever. Their compassion never ceases to amaze me (and sometimes overwhelm me).

3. A lot of them don't know how much they're getting screwed over. They think a film like *The Ugly Truth* is empowering, they read *He's Just Not That Into You*, and feed into the ideas that are designed to hurt them, they read *Cosmo* for guidance. It's easy for me to see that these things are all horrible but that's because I have a penis. I imagine that being a girl must make it so much harder to break away from these messages in popular culture. You're the target audience and women are usually the ones relaying the messages, which gives you the false impression that it's feminism or something. Hint: Feminism should never make you feel like a psycho bitch who is waiting for a boy to text her back.

4. Food is touchy. Food is a thing even if it's *not* a thing, you know? You don't have to be Karen Carpenter to say something disparaging about your body. You just have to read an issue of *Vogue*.

5. Throughout my life, I've always been drawn to the kind of energy women exude. I don't know how to

really describe it but I do know that it's truly mesmerizing to just watch girls get dressed in the morning, apply lipstick, walk down the street, laugh, cry, dance waving their hair around wildly, get naked, go swimming. I guess this kind of admission isn't surprising coming from a gay man. I remember studying my mom in the same way as a child. I would follow her around the house every day and watch her intently as she sprayed some perfume on her neck before she went out. I never dressed up in her clothes though. Promise.

6. Girls are tough but they're also fragile. It's an interesting duality. They'll be the first person to cry over a sentimental commercial but they also endure blood coming out of their vagina once a month, childbirth and being catcalled by a construction worker. They fight small battles every day and accept it as a part of their lives. It's funny to me that masculinity is all tied into your physical prowess. Because when it comes to dealing with the difficult things you can't just punch in the face, men will often shut down completely and become completely weak. Living in New York City or any other metropolitan city, gender roles are obviously less defined. For $1600 a month, you can live in a Michael Cera-induced New Masculinity bubble! Outside those city limits though, things can still be very caveman and scary.

7. Here is something that I've found sort of interesting. In my group of girlfriends, I've discovered that a lot of them are attracted to women. And not in an "I kissed a girl and my boyfriend liked it" Katy Perry kind of

way. Hell, they wouldn't even classify themselves as bisexual. They just like to do things like masturbate to lesbian porn or have sex with a girl occasionally. Is that, like, a thing or are all of my girlfriends just dipped into the extra freaky sauce?

16

The Definition of Love

You can stop taking quizzes in *Cosmo*. Here's what love really is.

Love is still wanting to hold someone after you climax. After the initial euphoria from the orgasm wears off, you're replaced with a sense of calm rather than a panic. You don't want to search for your clothes, scramble to find your keys and figure out the best way to tell them, "See ya later forever!" You're fine with chilling out in bed with the person and maybe ordering pad thai later.

Love is unattractive. It can expose our worst traits: Jealousy, irrational fears, heated anger; the gang's all here! While it can bring out compassion and tenderness, it can also make you behave like the ugliest version of yourself. That can be okay for a little while, but love with real longevity should be like a Xanax rather than an Adderall.

Love is not afraid to be schmaltzy. There's a reason why the most popular love songs are so lyrically simple. You can drown it in metaphors all you want but love usually boils down to, "You make me so happy. I want to hold your hand. I just want u 2 be mine 4ever!" You can be a 50-year-old linguistics professor at Columbia University and still find something to relate to in a Mariah Carey ballad if you're in love because the feelings are so universal. It's humbling, isn't it? No matter who you are or what your background is, love can reduce you to Mariah Carey mush.

Love is an all-consuming drug. It gives us these natural highs we've only read about in books or heard in songs. It's addictive. It's what keeps us going to bars, drinking glasses of wine, going to that stupid house party in Bushwick; it's all for the possibility of finding love. In the wrong hands, love can be dangerous and scary. If someone lacks a healthy foundation, love can kill. All of these crimes you read about in the newspapers are usually linked to passionate love. "I did it because I loved them just...too much."

Love is not what our parents had. In high school, you never wanted to think about your mother and father having once slept with people in the backseat of cars and feeling warm and happy. That would make it feel less special and young. It would make love have less to do with you when, EXCUSE ME, it has EVERYTHING to do with you.

Love is getting drunk with your significant other at a party and taking a cab home with your bodies intertwined. You feel safest in these moments, the most secure. Entering a social gathering with someone who loves you is the biggest security blanket. People leave the party as a parade of droopy expressions and sad cocktail dresses. But not you. "Sorry guys, I'm in love! I'm taking a car!"

Love is fucking stupid. Love is fucking smart. Love is about betraying yourself, of compromising your ideals for someone else's approval. That's actually the bad kind of love, but I guess it all blurs together when you're young or when you're old or when you don't love yourself.

Love is your significant other telling you about their favorite album and then making a point to fall in love with it on your own. Love is wondering why your better half loves certain things. You think you can find remnants of them in their favorite films, books and songs, but you usually can't.

Love is finding yourself feeling protective over someone else's well-being Love is being incensed with rage when someone or something has done your lover wrong.

Love is wanting your partner to cum. And if they can't, just say, "That's okay. I'm enjoying this." It might be bullshit, but they'll be orgasming in the next five minutes. Trust me.

Love isn't always marriage. Marriage is spending $60,000 so everyone can know that someone loves you. You know what's certainly not love? Debt. In some cases, love can be divorce.

Love is a back massage, a mindfuck, a hard cock, a pair of perfect breasts, of feeling unashamed about the cellulite on your body. Love is someone giving a shit about you enough to argue. Love is not passive. Love is "Don't fucking touch me right now." Love is "Who the FUCK were you talking to?" Love is sometimes hating yourself for a second. Love is hate. Period. Indifference is the real killer of love and the true antithesis.

When love leaves you, you should be lying on your bathroom floor with no resolve. You're smoking cigarettes in the bathtub and crying about everything bad that's ever happened.

Love is someone seeing the beauty in you and wanting to bask in it every day all day. Love is not guaranteed. We are not owed love. That's why when we get it, we know how lucky we are and hold on to it for dear life.

So, yeah. That's what love is. Anyone know where to get some?

17

How to Live in New York City

Move here when you're 18 or 22, maybe even 24. Come from somewhere else — the north, south, west, Xanadu — and come to realize that everyone living in New York is a transplant. Even the ones who grew up on the Upper East Side end up moving into a place downtown, which, as you'll soon discover, is like moving to a different city.

Discover the cruel and bizarre world of New York City real estate. End up spending an obscene amount of money on something called a broker's fee, first and last month's rent and a security deposit. Cry a little bit in the leasing office but remind yourself that you're so happy to be here.

Picture hearing a man playing the saxophone outside your bedroom window. End up hearing a lot of sirens instead. Figure it's okay because it's New York and you're still so happy to be here.

Go out to bars in the Lower East Side because the Internet told you so. Fall in love with a bar called, Max Fish, and always stay out till four in the morning. Eat a falafel and have someone pay for a cab back to your apartment. Watch the sun start to rise while going over the Williamsburg Bridge and feel like your life is becoming some kind of movie.

Eat bad pizza but trick yourself into believing it's good because it's made in New York. Do the same thing with bagels and sex.

Meet people who will be your best friends for three or four months. They'll help you transition into city life and take you to weird bars in Murray Hill. It will be like the blind leading the blind but once you get a firm grasp on things, you can stop returning their phone calls.

Watch your life in New York go through phases. Spend a summer in Fort Greene with a lover and get to know the neighborhood and its rhythms. Once the fling ends, forget the blocks, parks and restaurants ever existed and don't return unless you have to.

Encounter a lot of people crying in public. Watch an NYU student cry in Think Coffee, a business woman in midtown sob into her cellphone, an old man whimper on a stoop in Greenpoint. At first, it will feel very jarring but, like everything else, it will become normal. Have your first public cry in front of a Bank of America. Cry so hard and don't care if people are watching you. You pay good money to be able to cry in public.

Work long hours at a thankless job. Always be one step away from financial destitution. Marvel at how expensive New York is, how when you walk out the door, $20.00 immediately gets deleted from your wallet. Understand that even though no one has any money, everyone is privileged to live in New York City.

Go home for the holidays and run into old friends from high school. When you tell them that you live in New York, watch their eyes widen. They'll say, "Oh my god, New York? That's so crazy. I'm so jealous!" Have a blasé attitude about it but deep down inside, know they have good reason to be jealous.

Go home and feel relieved to be away from the energy of the city, that punishing 4:00 a.m. last call. Spend the first two days eating and sleeping, getting back to normal. Spend the last two days feeling anxious and ready to get back to your real home. Realize this city has you by the balls and isn't going to let you go.

Someday you might grow tired of it all though. You might start crying in public more often than you'd like, have a bad break-up and want to pack it all up.

Certain moments of living in the city will always stick out to you. Buying plums from a fruit vendor on 34th street and eating three of them on a long walk, the day you spent in bed with your best friend watching Tyra Banks, the amazing rooftop party you attended on a sweltering hot day in July. These memories might seem insignificant but they were all moments when you looked around the city and felt like you were a part of it all.

When you leave the city, you probably won't come back. Eventually your life in New York will seem so far away and sometimes you'll even wonder if it really happened. Don't worry. It did.

18

7 Signs You Can't Party As Much As You Used To

1. There was a period of time in your life when every night out seemed to end at 4 a.m. no matter what. It wasn't seen as being a big deal either. Like, duh, of course you're not going to go home till the bars close. Is there an alternative? Also, you had endless amounts of energy. You were never tired and even if you were, you could always power through it. You *never* surrendered to fatigue, are you kidding? Now, when you think of those nights, you immediately get flashbacks of a hangover and think, "How did I do that? Also, how did my party mentality change so quickly? I thought my thirties were my time to be a grandma, not 26."

2. You're picky about the kind of alcohol you drink. Recently, I was at a house party and I saw some dude just take giant swigs of whiskey out of a bottle. When I turned to my friend, I asked her, "Um, what is that guy doing?" and she responded, "Oh, he's 21," which explained everything. One of the major differences in

drinking at 21 versus, well, any other subsequent age is that you actually have had time to find alcohol you enjoy. Since you can't possibly get wasted every time you drink, you have to stick to what you like. Today I don't venture much outside of wine. In the summer, I'll drink margaritas and in the winter, I'll have hot toddies but that's about as adventurous I'll go. If I must, I'll get a gin and a tonic because, for some reason, I can't seem to ever get drunk off of them so it's a safe choice. Plus, I like that gin tastes like you're licking a battery. Oops!

3. You drink more often than you did in college but you in smaller increments. So, for example, in college I probably drank two to three nights a week but when I did, I would get WASTED. Like, puking in my apartment at 6 a.m. and losing my underwear wasted. Now, I probably drink five nights a week but I usually only have one or two drinks. I used to make fun of people who came home after a long day at work and were like, "I need to have a glass of wine to take the edge off!" but now I totally get it. Having one glass of wine just makes you feel normal again, which is sort of #dark but real nonetheless.

4. Again, seriously, nothing makes it more resoundingly clear that you can't party like you used to than drinking with anyone who's 21 or younger. You think you're cool, you think you can hang, and then you spend some time with a college student and realize that you're a fucking wimp when it comes to boozing — which, I mean, thank God. As fun as it was to be a borderline alcoholic for four years, it was also

incredibly painful physically, emotionally, and occasionally sexually.

5. You seriously start to worry about your looks. When a friend asks you why you can't come to an all-night rager, you simply send them a picture of Lindsay Lohan circa today and write, "Because I don't want this to happen to me."

6. Part of the reason why you went out so much and partied was because you suffered from Fear Of Missing Out or, as some people like to call it, F.O.M.O. As you get older, however, you realize that the only thing you miss out on after 2 a.m. is someone calling their coke dealer and a woman in a cupcake dress with smeared eye makeup crying in the bathroom.

7. You have hangovers that are sort of unreal. It didn't used to be this bad but now whenever you have four or five drinks, you can pretty much guarantee that the next day is going to be entirely deleted. It used to be fun spending your entire day in bed hungover watching Netflix and ordering Seamless but now it's just depressing. To feel better, you'll sit in the shower for an inordinate amount of time and let the water wash over you, feeling like a total screw up. It's a steep price to pay for one night of so-called fun.

19

How to be a 20-Something

Be really attractive. Your acne is gone, your face has matured without having wrinkles and everything on your body is lifted naturally. Eat bagels seven days a week, binge-drink and do drugs: you'll still look like a babe. When you turn thirty, it'll become a different story but that's, like, not for a really long time.

Reestablish a relationship with your parents. You don't live with them anymore (hopefully) so start to appreciate them as human beings with thoughts, flaws and feelings rather than soulless life ruiners who won't let you borrow their car.

Go from eating delicious food at your parents' house to eating Ragu tomato sauce over Barilla noodles. Develop an eating disorder to save money.

Move into an apartment on the corner of Overpriced and Dangerous. Sleep on a bare mattress with an Ikea comforter. Your mother talks to you about buying a top sheet and a duvet cover but feel like you're not mature enough to own something called "duvet."

Read the New York Times piece, "What Is It About 20-Somethings?" Feel exposed and humiliated. Share it on your Facebook with the caption: "Um…." Your friends will comment "Too real" and that will be the end of that.

Work at a coffee shop but feel hopeful about your career in advertising, writing, whatever. Remember that you're young and that the world is your oyster. Everything is possible, you still have so much to see and hear. You went to a good school and did good things. Figure if you're not going to be successful, who the hell is?

Date people who you know you'll never be able to love. See someone for three months for no other reason than because it's winter and you want to keep warm by holding another body. Date a Republican just so you can say you dated a Republican.

Eventually all these nobodies will make you crave a somebody. Have a real relationship with someone. Go on vacations together, exchange house keys, cry in their arms after a demoralizing day at work. Think about marrying them and maybe even get engaged. Regardless of the outcome, feel proud of yourself for being able to love someone in a healthy way.

Start your twenties with a lot of friends and leave with a few good ones. What happened? People faded away into their careers and relationships. Fights were had and never resolved. Shit happens.

Think of yourself at twenty and hanging out with people who didn't mean a thing to you. Think about writing papers, about being promiscuous, about trying new things. Think of yourself now and your face looking different and your body feeling different and how everything is just different.

Form the habits that will stick with you forever. Drink your coffee with two sugars and skim milk every morning. Buy a magazine every Friday. Enjoy spending money on candles, smoke pot on Saturdays, watch the television before bed.

Move into a bigger apartment on the corner of Mature and Gentrification and finally buy a duvet cover. Limit your drug-use. If you find yourself unable to do so, start to wonder if you have a problem.

Have your parents come to your place for Christmas. Set the table, make the ham, wear a sophisticated outfit; this will all mean so much at the time.

Think about having children when you stop acting like a child. This may not ever happen.

Maybe this is assuming too much. Maybe this is generalizing. Maybe society uses age as an unrealistic marker for growth. Maybe. Still feel the anxiety on your 30th birthday and think to yourself, "Oh shit, I'm no longer a 20-something."

20

What It Feels Like To Get Fucked In The Ass

Getting your ass penetrated should be a prerequisite for life because it's an experience that teaches humility and encourages teamwork. After the deed, you see your fellow man in a whole new empathetic light, the kind of light that's humanizing, curbs any further judgments and could possibly end wars. It's like, "You just let me put my penis in your ass and move it in and out for an hour. God bless you, you wonderful angel. Take this 'get out of jail free' card. You've earned it!"

The only people who aren't getting fucked in the ass are straight men. Lesbians use dildos, straight girls get drunk and acquiesce to their boyfriend's requests, and gay guys, well, we sort of invented anal sex. If *Jersey Shore* has "Gym, Tan, Laundry," gay men have "Gym, Tan, Anal." As I've discussed before, the male equivalent of a G-spot rests in our prostate so the incentive to get someone's dick in our ass ASAPular is that much greater.

But here's some real talk for you. Anal sex is kind of the biggest deal ever. When my friends tell me stories about doing it with some random they met at a bar, I'm completely stunned.

The act is so intense and delicate that I could never give my asshole to just anybody. Entrance is only granted to V.I.P.'s—Very Important Penises. But this is something the gay community doesn't always see ass-to-ass on. Some only have anal sex in monogamous relationships and consider oral sex to be intercourse. With others, however, it's like throwing a hot dog down a hallway. Anal is like the oxygen they need to breathe.

I'm going to try to put the feeling of anal sex into words so you can get an idea of how crazysexyintense it is. First of all, anal sex cannot be an on-the-fly decision. If I'm getting fucked in the ass, I need to know way in advance so I can prepare properly. The guy needs to send me a private Facebook event invitation titled, "Ryan O'Connell gets fucked in the ass." with a set date and time. I can then have the luxury of choosing "Attending", "Maybe Attending" or "Not Attending." If I choose to attend, I need to start doing some serious yoga to Sade or Enya. When that's done, I'll give a pep talk to my asshole and be like, "Hey babe! I know you've been in retirement or whatever, but you need to get ready because something's coming to an orifice near you. Don't hate me! You'll like it. And don't try any funny business tonight. I'll be mortified if you-know-what happens!" After chilling your asshole out, you kind of need to go in the shower and fuck yourself with your finger. You don't want it to be too tight because then it runs the risk of being very painful. While loosening things up, take this opportunity to clean things up. You don't want to go into the experience feeling insecure about the state of your ass so be thorough in your examination.

Fast forward to the main event. It's imperative that the guy who's going to be penetrating me is trustworthy and gentle, and not an asshole. Assholes don't mix with my asshole. I'm going to be getting in sexual positions where my body will look fleshy and revolting. It will seem like I've magically gained 20 pounds somewhere for no real reason so this guy needs to be understanding of everything. Hopefully his dong won't be too huge either because that can become difficult to manage.

When he goes in, it's going to feel strange at first. Actually, anal sex always feels strange. It's hard to explain but the whole thing just feels wrong. I don't mean that in a moralistic or bad way. I mean, it just literally feels unnatural because you're using an exit as an entrance. Funnily enough though, that's how you derive a lot of enjoyment from it. The unnatural feeling enhances the pleasure. You know how when you watch people getting fucked in gay porn, there's all this moaning, and you're just like, "yeah, right. they're acting"? I can't be for sure obviously but I don't think they are. When a penis enters your ass, a moan involuntarily escapes your lips. Just try not to be loud. I dare you. You have little control over it, which makes the experience even hotter.

When he starts to really fuck you, it gets very overwhelming. You're making noises you didn't even know existed and the whole thing is just blowing your mind. All of these sensations are just making you feel so vulnerable, and you're staring at the dude (well depending on the position) and you usually feel some warm and fuzzies towards them. You also might think the way they're fucking you is incredibly hot and primal and oh my god you've never wanted them so badly before! You want them to fuck you so hard and jesus christ, where is all of this coming from?! You just want to get fucked, you know?! Fuck me!

You're writhing and shaking and everything that's happening feels so dirty and hideous kinky. You feel like this is what you were built to do—get fucked. It just feels so right and back to basics. You might never feel more like an animal than you do in these moments of getting fucked in the ass. There are no more nuances to humans, no more complexities. It has just boiled down to wanting to get fucked.

It's impossible for me not to feel close to someone when all of this is happening. There's a bond that develops that makes it impossible for it to happen with men who don't mean a thing to me. Anal sex is a special thing. I'm unwilling to perceive it as casual. I feel like putting someone's P in a V is more manageable and impersonal, but what do I know? I just know that it feels crazy to get fucked in the ass. It hurts, it feels good, it feels wrong, it feels right. It's a dick going deep into your ass. It's a connection. I recommend it to all.

21

5 Signs You Definitely Don't Have Your Shit Together

1. You can't cook

Is it just me or does everyone else find so-called "easy" cooking recipes to be the hardest thing imaginable? I just read one for a chicken soup that you're supposed to be able to make even when you're sick and feel like dying, but it still seemed impossible to me. Like, I could NEVER make this chicken soup even if I was at my best. All these "cooking for beginners" recipes are like, "So just use some spare chicken stock you have lying around in the fridge and, you know, throw some parsnips and figs in there, and voila, you have the most simple version of soup. A blind man could do it!" Uh, no. I don't even know what chicken stock is. Is it something you can invest in on Wall Street? All I have in my fridge right now is old take out soup, marinara sauce, Thin Mints, and Vicodin (best served chilled, obvs). Tell me what I can make with those ingredients, Rachael Ray!

2. You have no idea what to do when you're sick

Last month, I somehow managed to develop two abscesses on my face, except I didn't know they were abscesses. I just thought they were super painful zits. So I left them alone for a while until I started experiencing random fever dreams in the middle of the night and my skin felt like it was getting hit with a jackhammer. Then I was like, "Weird! Maybe I should check this out?" So I ran screaming into the arms of my dermatologist, who told me that I had developed two cysts and that an infection has spread to my lymph nodes. "You're really sick," she told me. "Have you not noticed?" Um, not really. I'm not one of those people who is in tune with their body. We don't have a natural rhythm developed. In fact, I don't even think we're on speaking terms. Occasionally, I'll text it and be like, "Hey babe, what's the deal with this headache I'm currently experiencing? Do I have a brain tumor?" And then my body will text me back and say, "No, you idiot. Just take some Advil and leave me alone!" Whenever I actually do get sick, I have no idea what to do so I just pretend it's not happening. Great system, no? The key to living a long life!

3. Gay mermaids are getting into relationships and you're still single

The most disturbing thing about this gay merman on the latest episode of TLC's *My Strange Obsession* is not the fact that he literally swims around in water with a fake fin attached to his body. It's that he actually has A BOYFRIEND. You guys, a gay guy who's convinced he's a mythical creature is off the market and I don't get it. Is this some kinky sex fetish thing? It must be, right? People don't just date mermen unless they want to fuck a fin, correct? Ugh. You know who also has a boyfriend?

Jessica Simpson's creepy as fuck dad! Yeah, he was gay for five minutes before he hooked up with some meth-y 19-year-old in West Hollywood! While I would never want that for myself, I still can't help but be disturbed that Joe Simpson and a gay mermaid have boyfriends and not me. Clearly I don't have my shit together. Clearly I'm doing something wrong if gay fish are getting laid but I'm not.

4. You can't put a duvet cover on to save your life

Last weekend I went and bought a new down comforter and duvet cover because mine was five years old and torn to shreds. So I go to Crate & Barrel feeling like the ultimate sophisticated adult, purchase the aforementioned items, and prance on home feeling very accomplished and together. "I bought new bed things! I bought things that go on my bed! Looks like I've reached my adult quota for the next year." My euphoria was short-lived, however, when I realized that I would actually have to put the duvet cover on my new comforter. This is probably the least favorite chore for everybody but to me, it's an impossible task. I tried for an hour to get that motherfucker comforter into the diva duvet but the two weren't having it. They weren't connecting or seeing eye-to-eye. Finally, I had to call up my friend who's 4 foot 11 and bribe her with a free dinner at Red Lobster if she would get INSIDE the duet cover and sort out the comforter. It worked. My friend came over, rolled around inside the duvet cover wrestling with the comforter, got it all evened out, and then we went for cheddar biscuits. But, like, I can't be doing this forever, right? Eventually my friends will be married with kids and won't have the time to help me with the duvet cover, no matter how many free dinners at exclusive chain restaurants I tempt them with!

5. You can't keep anything alive

For my birthday, my sister got me a beautiful plant that you only had to water once every 30 days. It somehow managed to die in under a month, which I didn't think was possible, but I guess it took one look at its new environment and was like, "BRB, going to kill myself."

22

The Complete Guide To Having Feelings

The "I HATE EVERYONE" Feeling

This is one of the most common feelings to ever exist and can be triggered by a variety of different things, including but not limited to: spending too much time on the internet, talking to a stupid person, watching a fat person eat a hot fudge sundae, or finding out that someone you know is becoming more successful than you. There is no way to really get rid of this feeling other than to just, you know, love yourself. But that's really hard to do. To love yourself is to know yourself and who the HELL really knows who they are?

Double this feeling: Lurk people from high school on Facebook, read Internet commenters, go to a fashion party and talk to a barely literate girl named Sophie who just made $50,000 from DJing a party in Dubai.

The "I'm going to the airport in a cab" Feeling

This feeling originates from having watched too many episodes of *The Hills*. It feels like an epic movie moment, like you're leaving behind your life and starting over — even if you're actually just going away for two days.

Double this feeling: Play an epic song on your iPod like "All My Friends" by LCD Soundsystem or "Teenage Wasteland" by The Who, and stare at the window longingly for the duration of the ride. Fall into a complete daze and only come to when your cab driver tells you that you've arrived.

The "I'm sitting down in the shower" Feeling

Some of your best thoughts will come to you when you're sitting down in the shower and letting the water wash over you. You're at peace, away from everything, and you can finally just let your feelings move around and do their job. A shower epiphany is the best kind of epiphany, in my opinion. Well, the ones you have while driving in a car late at night or on a park bench can be pretty great too.

Double this feeling: Stare at your pruned fingers and then your penis. Sigh audibly and dunk your head lazily underneath the shower nozzle.

The "I'm laying down in bed and staring at the ceiling" Feeling

Nothing opens the emotional floodgates faster than laying down on your bed and staring at your blank walls. It will make you feel like a 5-year-old who's been sent to bed without dessert. Your feelings will run the gamut, everywhere from "I'm tired" to "I hate my life" to "Maybe I should just masturbate…"

Double this feeling: Have your roommate walk in on your brooding fest and feel very uncomfortable, like they just caught you with your pants down. Burn incense.

The "I just got laid" Feeling

The "I just got laid" feeling is coveted by many. We want to experience it all the time, we want to drown in it, but we can't always get what we want now can we? When you do get your wish granted though, you'll do strange things like decide to walk home in a vicious snowstorm or call your grandma. You will feel complete for the next 37 hours. You might even clean your room.

Double this feeling: Have sex with someone else a day after. Look at yourself naked in the mirror for five minutes. Maybe six if you look thin and the sex was great.

The "I want to get drunk and/or do drugs" Feeling

Depending on who you are, your proclivity toward addiction, and how crappy your life is, you might experience this feeling anywhere from once a month to five times a day. It will make you feel weak and desperate, like you have unhealthy coping mechanisms. You will feel the urge to combat this with feelings of "I want to be a better person and not give into this self-destructive pattern." You will, in all likelihood, still end up drinking and/or doing drugs. Ha ha!

Double this feeling: Get dumped, get into a fight with your boyfriend or, even worse, be really bored.

The "I'm very lucky" Feeling

This feeling rarely happens because having perspective can make life less fun but when it does occur to you that you live a pretty good life, you will smile for the next 10 minutes, at least. You'll pat yourself on the back for being so self-aware and then spend 30 dollars on dinner without feeling guilt which, by the way, is one of the most useless feelings ever and has the highest calorie content. Don't ever feel guilt! Be a sociopath!

Double this feeling: Watch *Precious* or read about some girl with no legs who's on welfare in Stockton, California.

The "Everyone has their shit together but me!" Feeling

Feelings of inadequacies spill over into about 60% of the things you feel every day. It can be triggered by the morning after a one-night stand or the fact that you just spent your last 20 dollars on weed. I mean, there are a lot of opportunities for you to feel bad about yourself. You don't have to look too far. Trust me.

Double this feeling: Bring coke to a party and have everyone decline when you ask if they want some.

The "I'm fat" Feeling

Everyone feels fat at some point, even people who are most definitely skinny. This feeling occurs most prevalently during the summertime when you're forced to be naked and, thus, more aware of your body.

Double this feeling: Be a gay man or a girl. Try on a pair of jeans at a hipster clothing store. Be best friends with someone who's anorexic. Read fashion magazines. Eat over the sink at midnight. Be actually fat.

The "I'm in love, bitch!" Feeling

If you have the opportunity to feel what it's like to be in love, you will understand that it is the best feeling ever. Like, every other feeling can suck it. This one is numero uno. Bye.

Double this feeling: Have your person give you a scalp massage, two blowjobs a day, and feed you Thai food in bed. Be too in love to go on the internet. Learn the art of compromise. Feel like your lover is a bulletproof vest over your heart. (YEAH, THIS FEELING IS THAT GAY.)

The "I think I'm falling out of love with you" Feeling

This feeling can happen anytime after the "I'm in love, bitch!" feeling. Sometimes it never happens but that's like super rare. Only Rita Wilson and Tom Hanks have that. You could experience this feeling consistently or just for brief moments like when the person you love eats the last popsicle or poops with the door open.

Double this feeling: Cheat on them. Tell them lies. Imagine their "O" face over and over again while talking to your mother.

The "Wait, why are we friends again?" Feeling

This feeling is super sad albeit very common. It can happen anytime really. One day you can just wake up and forget the reason why you liked someone. You'll be having lunch together and realize that the glue has come undone. They're a stranger now.

Double this feeling: Go on a weeklong vacation with this person.

The "I think I have too many feelings" Feeling

This epiphany comes to you when you find yourself crying at commercials for cat food.

Double this feeling: Write a comprehensive list of all the feelings you experience on a semi-regular basis. Then have a lot of feelings about it.

23

A Phone Conversation with James Franco

There's something about James Franco. Whether he's dressing up in drag, enrolling in four graduate schools or just acting really weird and high, he manages to keep the public interested in whatever he's doing. In this celebrity age of calculated Disney starlets and PR sound bites, he's an anomaly — someone who is willing to take risks (I don't envy his publicist) and shock the world. At this point, liking his films or his art seems to be almost beside the point. More than an actor/student/writer/artist, James Franco has become famous for being James Franco–a refreshing and necessary presence in pop culture. It also doesn't hurt that he's super hot. It's a known fact that super hot people can get away with anything they want.

Well, pretty much anything. Franco's latest creative endeavor, a collection of short stories entitled *Palo Alto* (Scribner), really tested the limits to my love. It's not that it was downright terrible. The book definitely shows glimmers of promise but, as a whole, it comes across as very "student work." I just graduated college so I get it. But I also don't have a book deal.

Thought Catalog tried to interview Franco about his book but quickly hit a wall. So we just decided to make one up.

Thought Catalog: Hello, James Franco. How are you? What are you up to?

James Franco: Great, man. Right now, I'm translating *Catcher In The Rye* into Latin for fun and talking to Ron Howard on video chat.

TC: Sounds like a blast.

JF: Latin is really magical.

TC: Right. So, you wrote a book....

JF: I did, yeah.

TC: What was the writing process like?

JF: It was pretty organic. I mean, this one night at UCLA, my friend Samantha and I were on Adderall and feeling super creative. And I was telling her these stories about growing up in Palo Alto. Samantha finally was like, "You should write a short story collection about this and call it Palo Alto." So I thought about it and went to Pinkberry and let the idea marinate. And went back to my apartment and wrote the whole thing.

TC: In one night?

JF: Yeah, man. It was like I was possessed. It was like I was pregnant and needed to give birth to these stories, you know?

TC: I guess. So how did you go about getting it published?

JF: Well, I called Esquire magazine and was like, "I wrote these stories. Do you want to publish one?" And they're like, "Duh, James Franco." And then I texted Scribner Publishing my stories and they wrote back, "OMG. Loves it. Publishing it in October. XOXO."

TC: Oh. You're really hot, James Franco.

JF: Thanks.

TC: Can we, like, have sex?

JF: Maybe. You're a dude, right?

TC: Yeah.

JF: Only if we can videotape it and then submit it to The Whitney.

TC: Cool.

JF: (Silence)

TC: So the stories all seem to be about bored teenagers in Palo Alto, would that be an accurate description?

JF: I see it more as commentary on the rampant consumerism of the closeted post-modern era. But, yeah. Your description works fine.

TC: It's also about random acts of violence. People die a lot, get in car crashes, get shot.

JF: Yeah, I like that shit.

TC: You also touch on race a bit.

JF: I do? Where?

TC: Well, in one story, "Chinatown (in three parts)," a teenage boy hooks up with a half-Vietnamese classmate named Pam.

JF: Pam, I love that.

TC: Right. And afterwards, this boy pawns her off on all of his friends and she sleeps with them, for no apparent reason. At one point, they even gangbang her and she's sodomized by a carrot. They give her the nickname, Chinatown.

JF: Oh my god, she DOES get sodomized by a carrot. I remember that. That's insane. Tell me more.

TC: Well, she eventually stops sleeping with them but four months later, the boy gets arrested by a "Mexican cop" who wants to charge him with rape. Apparently Pam went to the police? I don't know. You weren't very clear on that. Anyways, he gets off because it was consensual (I guess) and the boy never talks to Pam again. You end the story with: "When we got older, I did things with my life and she did things with her life."

JF: That sounds beautiful. Who wrote that? I need to get their info.

TC: You did, James Franco.

JF: Oh my god, you're right. I'm sorry. I'm distracted by Ron Howard. We're playing charades on video chat right now. He's such a maniac.

TC: So, in the story, Pam is very much "the other" and she's essentially sexually abused by all of these boys. The interesting thing is that we get no insight into Pam's thought process or her character. Was that intentional or just bad writing?

JF: Oh, bad writing for sure. Sorry, man. Like I said, Adderall. One night. You know.

TC: You never had a book editor?

JF: Sort of. It was just this gay guy who took me to lunch sometimes and would, like, touch me underneath the table. He never gave me actual notes. Except he did tell me once to wear more blue because it would contrast well with my eyes.

TC: I don't know what to say, James Franco.

JF: (Silence)

TC: Um, in another story called, "Lockheed," a lonely girl meets a boy she likes at a house party and then-woops-he dies in a fight. Like I mentioned earlier, there's a lot of hate and violence in this book. Do you see the youth of Palo Alto as being more angry than most?

JF: I don't really know. I think I'm just attracted to violent things and, um, the work should just speak for itself.

TC: Isn't that the same thing you said about your films, *Tristan + Isolde* and *Whatever It Takes*?

JF: I can't confirm or deny. You're a horse!

TC: What?

JF: Sorry. Charades, again.

TC: OK, let me just wrap it up with one last question. Are you gay?

JF: I don't know. People will have to read the book to find out.

TC: But it's not a memoir.

JF: Yes, it is.

TC: No, it's not.

JF: Yes, it is.

TC: No.

JF: Yes. (DIALTONE)

24

Why He Will Never Love You

You're kissing this boy right now. You're kissing him and he's kissing you. Actually, he's not *really* kissing you. He might be moving his mouth in the correct ways and moaning but he's gone. He's not here right now. Leave a message at the beep. You're kissing his mouth and soon you'll be kissing his neck and finally you'll be kissing his cock but you mustn't forget something: you are never kissing his heart. Not even close.

Remember that this boy is an asshole and he has been sent here on Earth to destroy open-hearted people like you. He's here to tarnish your self-esteem and leave you in pieces. He's here to be a chapter in your book, and you a pithy footnote in his. You will have two wildly different interpretations of the relationship and when the stories don't match up, it will make you feel like you're losing your mind, that you really are the delusional psycho he's painted you out to be. Don't worry. You're not. You've just met the boy who's supposed to destroy people like you.

He doesn't love you like you love him. Your love is this big, beaming light and his love is that dead gnat on the ground. But for right now, I guess he's yours. He's renting out his body to you for the night as a courtesy. At first, you'll feel so glad that he did. "Oh thank you," you'll cry out at his feet. "Thank you for letting me having you for this brief moment of ecstasy." When it's all over though, you'll hate him. Just like that. You'll have arrived at his house with such promise and vigor to change him but he sucked you dry yet again. He wanted you to know that it will never be the way you want it to be, that he will never be the way you want him to be. And now you know. Again. Hold on to this knowledge until you develop the amnesia that'll keep you coming back for more.

Rule number one: Never believe anything anyone tells you in bed. Beds are safe spaces where lies take root and grow, grow, grow all the way to the ceiling until, suddenly, you'll find yourself surrounded by nothing but lies. Overgrown weeds you have to whack your way through just to get out of bed. Some people never leave though. Some people are comforted by the lies so they sleep with them every night.

This can't be you. You have to get out of bed. As fast as you can.

He will say sweet things to you in bed, things you can't believe are coming out of his mouth. It's easy to say those sweet things when you're lying next to a naked body. Try telling them again when you're in a turtleneck and have a cold and ice is sticking to your face. It's a lot harder then.

He leaves your bed and the second he does, the spell is broken. Even the way he dresses — casually, lazily, dismissive — will be enough to make your heart sink again. "Come back to bed," you'll say, patting the sheets.

"I can't. Sorry. Got stuff to do today."

He fills you up just to deplete you later.

You can only have him in bed. Outside of it, you can't have anything. You're stripped of your rights.

Don't act surprised. You know better than to act surprised.

Just get out. He's a dead-end. He won't let you love him. Never will. You're loving brick and mortar. Not a human body. You can love more than a wall. Hell, you need to love more than a wall.

He leaves. You lay in bed just a little longer so you can linger with his smells. You decide that you hate him.

He hates you.

No, wait. That's still not right.

You hate yourself.

THOUGHT
CATALOG
Books

Thought Catalog Books is a publishing house owned by The Thought & Expression Company, an independent media group based in Brooklyn, NY. Founded in 2010, we are committed to facilitating thought and expression. We exist to help people become better communicators and listeners in order to engender a more exciting, attentive, and imaginative world.

Visit us on the web at
www.thoughtcatalogbooks.com and *www.collective.world*.